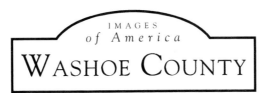

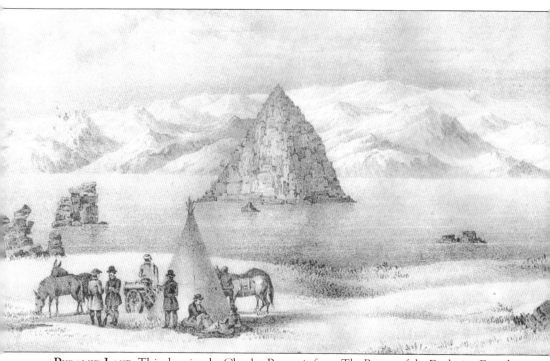

PYRAMID LAKE. This drawing by Charles Preuss is from *The Report of the Exploring Expeditions to the Rocky Mountains in the year 1842 and to Oregon and North California in the years 1843-'44* by Captain John C. Fremont. Fremont wrote: "This striking feature suggested a name for the lake; and I called it Pyramid lake." (Author's collection.)

ON THE COVER: DEEP HOLE RANCH. James and John Raser with sisters Minnie and Ellen are playing musical instruments at the Deep Hole Ranch that was part of the Gerlach Livestock Company in 1890. James worked as the superintendent for the ranch while John worked as a range rider. (Nevada Historical Society, wa00488.)

IMAGES of America
WASHOE COUNTY

Joyce M. Cox

Copyright © 2011 by Joyce M. Cox
ISBN 978-0-7385-8168-2

Published by Arcadia Publishing
Charleston, South Carolina

Printed in the United States of America

Library of Congress Control Number: 201929731

For all general information, please contact Arcadia Publishing:
Telephone 843-853-2070
Fax 843-853-0044
E-mail sales@arcadiapublishing.com
For customer service and orders:
Toll-Free 1-888-313-2665

Visit us on the Internet at www.arcadiapublishing.com

*To my husband Greg Cox, son Alex Cox, sisters Janice Weide
and Carolyn Crowson, and my father and mother, Al and Woodie
Crowson. Thanks for all of your support and love through the years.
This book is also dedicated to my dog Bannor,
who passed away while I was writing it.*

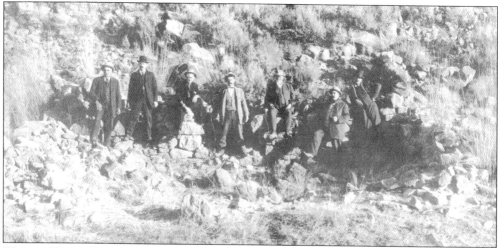

WASHOE VALLEY PIONEERS. Early pioneers of Washoe Valley are standing on ruins in the valley in 1910. Daniel C. Wheeler is the third from the left, and R.O. Martin is fifth from left. Wheeler was an early sheep rancher in the Truckee Meadows. (Nevada Historical Society, wa00757.)

Contents

Acknowledgments		6
Introduction		7
1.	Early People	9
2.	A Fertile Valley	21
3.	Rush to Washoe	45
4.	Railroads, Highways, and Airplanes	73
5.	Schools, Churches, and Picnics	99
6.	Water and Power	117
Bibliography		127

Acknowledgments

I would like to thank those who helped me: the staff of the downtown branch of the Washoe County Library for the use of their Nevada collections and their newspaper archive database; Sheryln Hayes-Zorn, Michael Maher, Heidi Englund, and Lee Brumbaugh at the Nevada Historical Society for the use of their library and manuscript collections and their fantastic photograph collection; Jeffrey Kintop at the Nevada State Library and Archives for reading and correcting my manuscript; library services staff of the Nevada State Library and Archives for use of their Nevada and Government Documents collections; Debbie Seracini of Arcadia Publishing for helping me through the writing and selection of photographs; Sue Ballew for advice on photographs and writing my book; and Dan Webster and Cindy Southerland for the use of their Nevada collections. Thank you to my husband, Gregory M. Cox; my son, Alex Cox; and my sister Janice Weide for reading and editing the manuscript. Thanks to all who donated their photographs: Julie Duewel, photographer at the Nevada Department of Transportation; Lee Brumbaugh, curator of photography at the Nevada Historical Society; Dan Webster; Cindy Southerland of Southerland Studios; and Susan Searcy at the Nevada State Library and Archives.

All images used in this book were obtained from the collections of the Nevada Historical Society, Nevada Department of Transportation, Nevada State Library and Archives, Cindy Southerland, and Dan Webster.

INTRODUCTION

Washoe County is in the extreme northwestern part of the state of Nevada. Its history from 1863 to 1968 is depicted through the photographs and prints in this book. Washoe County was one of the nine original counties of the Nevada Territory in 1861. In 1864, when Nevada became a state, Washoe County was combined with part of Roop (now Lake) County to cover the area including Pyramid and Winnemucca Lakes. Later, in 1884, it was combined with the remaining parts of Roop County to reach its current area bordering Oregon on the north and California on the west. Washoe County covers 6,608 square miles, including Incline Village and Crystal Bay on Lake Tahoe in its southwest corner, Gerlach near the Black Rock Desert, and Wadsworth, Nixon, and Sutcliff near Pyramid Lake. Reno is the current county seat.

Washoe County is part of the Great Basin, a high, dry desert with mountain ranges and valleys, grasses and sagebrush, and large empty spaces. Hunters and trappers may have come through the area in the 1820s, but the earliest written records were of John Bidwell (1841), "Old Bill" Williams (1843), and John C. Fremont (1843). Fremont's expedition crossed the southern Oregon border into northern Nevada in December 1843. His group discovered the hot springs near Gerlach on January 6, 1844, named Pyramid Lake on January 10, and gave the name Salmon Trout River to what is now the Truckee River on January 16. Fremont camped next to Pyramid Lake and described it as "a sheet of green water set like a gem in the mountains."

Washoe County's name was derived from the Wassau (Washo or Washoe) Indian tribe, a hunting and gathering people who fished and hunted in the summer at Lake Tahoe and spent winter and spring in Carson Valley, Douglas Valley, and Washoe Valley. The Northern Paiute tribe living in eastern California, western Nevada, and southern Oregon fished the cui-ui at Pyramid Lake. The Pyramid Lake Paiute Reservation, 35 miles northeast of Reno, was set aside by the Bureau of Indian Affairs in 1859. President Grant issued an executive order establishing the reservation in 1874.

Emigrants traveled through the area on their way to California by following the Applegate-Lassen Trail, the Nobles Route, and the Truckee River Route. The ill-fated Donner Party passed through Washoe County in 1846. Many of the California-bound travelers who stayed built homes, ranches, and businesses in the tree-filled valley that became known as the Truckee Meadows. The Clark family, the first settlers near Franktown in Washoe Valley in 1852, wanted to name their homestead the Garden of Eden. H.H. Jamison set up a trading post in the Truckee Meadows in 1852. A reporter for the *Nevada State Journal* in November 1896 described the Truckee Meadows as the "first spot of beauty and rest beyond the lonely and barren desert. Last stopping place of gold hunters' pilgrimage; the oasis beautiful, lying at the feet of the mighty Sierras [sic], miles of weaving meadows, through whose sheen of grassy verdure the breezes ripple on iridescent colors."

Farmers and lumbermen in Washoe County found a market for their lumber, timber, cordwood, hay, alfalfa, and other agricultural products in Virginia City and Gold Hill after the discovery of the Comstock Lode in 1859. The Washoe Valley towns of Franktown, Ophir, and Washoe

City had farms and ranches, sawmills, and quartz mills. Galena, east of Steamboat Hills, was a timber producer for the Comstock mines. When the Comstock boom ended in the 1880s, many of the workers migrated back to Washoe County to mine, farm, ranch, or become merchants. These new settlers brought new commerce by building bridges, toll roads, hotels, saloons, grist mills, schools, post offices, churches, hospitals, and cemeteries. Gold and silver were mined near Gerlach, Washoe City, Olinghouse, Peavine (Poeville), and Wedekind. Tungsten, copper, and lead were sought near Olinghouse and Leadville.

In 1868, the Central Pacific Railroad, part of the first transcontinental railroad, was built through Washoe County. The Truckee River towns of Reno, Verdi, Mogul, Wadsworth, and Sparks were founded or expanded as railroad stations. Wadsworth became a freight center for the mining camps in Esmeralda, Nye, and Churchill Counties. Construction of the Virginia & Truckee Railroad in 1871 connected Virginia City mines to Carson City, eliminating the need for the sawmills and quartz mills in Washoe City, Franktown, and Ophir. In 1872, the Virginia & Truckee Railroad was extended to Reno, connecting the Virginia City mines to the Central Pacific Railroad. Additional commerce and tourists came with the building of the Lincoln and Victory Highways in the early 20th century.

In 1931, the Nevada Legislature legalized gambling and shortened the residency requirement for divorces. These new industries helped Washoe County through the Depression. Tourism, along with gaming, became the major industry in the county. Hotels and casinos were built for tourists coming to gamble. Divorce ranches, or dude ranches, were opened throughout the county to house people for the six-week residency period. Warehousing became another important industry in 1949 after the Nevada legislature passed the free-port law that exempted warehoused merchandise from personal property tax.

Washoe County grew since its formation from an estimated 1,613 people in 1861 to 421,407 people in 2010. It was the most populated county in Nevada from 1890 to 1950. The small towns of Washoe City, Franktown, Jumbo, Galena, Olinghouse, Vya, Flanigan, Leadville, and Poeville declined to near extinction over the years. Reno and Sparks are the population hubs, while Gerlach, Empire, Wadsworth, and Nixon have populations between 500 and 800. Incline Village and Verdi have populations of 9,952 and 2,949, respectively. Lumber mills are no longer part of the economy and few ranches remain. Mining and quarrying in the county is predominately for sand, gravel, and dimension stone rather than for gold or silver. Today the largest employers are in education and health services, casinos and hotels, and manufacturing and warehousing. Residents and tourists coming to Washoe County can participate in outdoor activities such as hiking, white-water rafting, kayaking, water skiing, fishing, and golfing in the summer and hunting and snow skiing in the winter. Annual events include the National Championship Air Races, Greater Reno Balloon Races, Hot August Nights, Reno Tahoe Open, Reno Rodeo, Street Vibrations, Burning Man, and Artown.

One

EARLY PEOPLE

The first people living in the northern Great Basin arrived between 12,000 and 15,000 years ago. Some traveled through the area looking for less hostile environments, while others stayed to become part of the Numa (Numu), Washeshu, and Newe (Paiute, Washoe, and Shoshone) tribes. The Indians of the northern Great Basin traveled throughout the area gathering food and material for clothing and shelter. Land near Pyramid Lake was set aside as the Pyramid Lake Indian Reservation in 1859 and was formalized by President Grant in 1874. The Reno Sparks Indian Colony was established in 1936.

Hunters and trappers passed through in the 1820s. The explorer John C. Fremont entered High Rock Canyon in northern Washoe County in 1843 and camped along the Truckee River near Pyramid Lake on January 10, 1844. The immigrant party led by Elisha Stevens, accompanied by a Paiute Indian named Truckee, followed the Truckee River from Wadsworth west through the Truckee Meadows to Donner Lake, establishing the California Trail. The Applegate-Lassen Trail passed through the High Rock Canyon on the way to California. The Clark family settled in Franktown in 1852 but left after only a year. In the spring of 1852, H.H. Jamison, a Mormon settler, came to the eastern Truckee Meadows to set up the first trading post near the mouth of the Truckee River Canyon. Jamison sold supplies and cattle to emigrants going through the meadows to California. John F. Stone and Charles C. Gates built a trading post in Glendale, in what is now Sparks, and established a ferry across the Truckee River in 1857.

The Comstock gold rush in 1859 in nearby Virginia City and Gold Hill brought more people to the area. Sawmills and quartz mills were built in Washoe Valley, and ranchers in all of Washoe County provided agricultural products for the mines on the Comstock Lode.

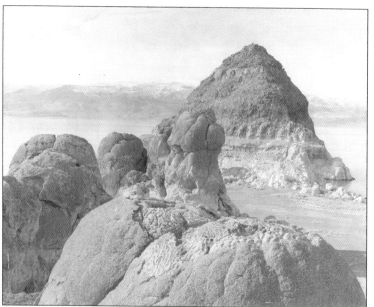

PYRAMID IN PYRAMID LAKE. The Pyramid Lake Indian Reservation covers 322,000 acres, including the 2,000 acres of Pyramid Lake. Tufa formations of calcium carbonate scattered around the border of the lake form the pyramid, the Great Stone Mother, and the needles. The Paiute Indians called the pyramid *Wono* and the lake *Cui-Ui Panunadu*. (Nevada Historical Society, wa00360.)

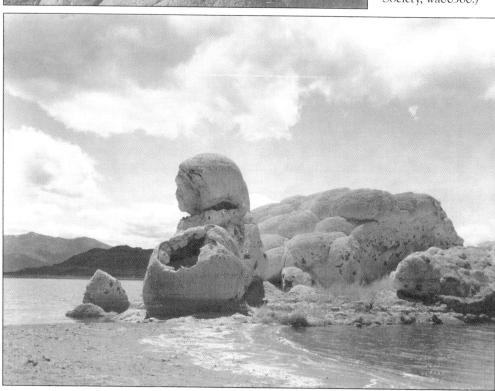

GREAT STONE MOTHER. According to the Paiute Indian legend, the Great Mother and Great Father lived in the valley that is now Pyramid Lake with their sons. The sons became the leaders of the people that occupied the area and began fighting with each other. When the sons could not be persuaded to stop fighting, the Great Father sent them away. The Great Mother sat on the hillside with her basket while her tears filled up the lake and she turned to stone. (Nevada Historical Society, WA-00365.)

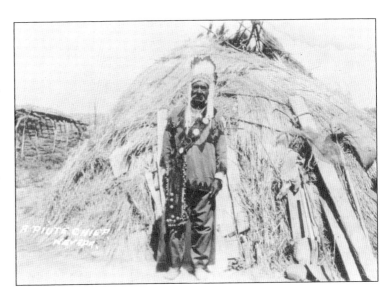

PAIUTE KANI. The winter dwelling known as a *kani* was a dome-shaped house covered with cattail or wild grass mats over a frame of juniper poles. The house was from 8 to 15 feet in diameter with a smoke hole in the top and a doorway on the side. Juniper branches and dirt were placed over the mats for protection from the cold. (Nevada Historical Society, eth00038.)

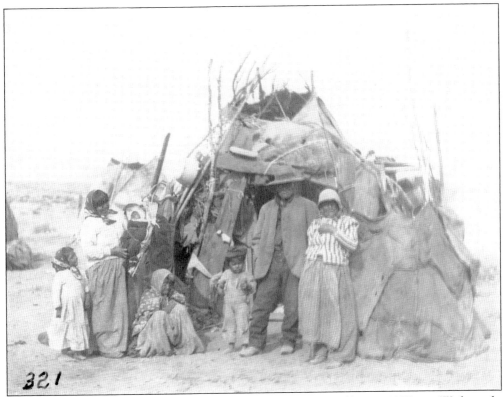

PAIUTE FAMILY. A Paiute family is shown with their conical-shaped *kani* in 1907 near Wadsworth. In the early 1900s, the dome-shaped design was changing to one with a flat roof framed with willows and covered with burlap bags and carpet remnants that were obtained from the white settlers. (Nevada Historical Society, eth00321.)

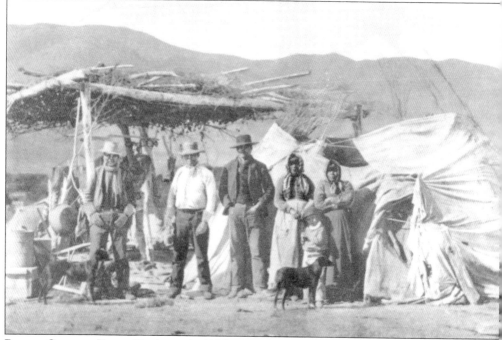

PAIUTE CAMP IN RENO. By the early 1900s, Paiutes were living on the outskirts of Reno and Wadsworth hoping to find work with the white settlers since there was no work on the Pyramid Lake Indian Reservation. Paiute men and women would work at housecleaning, laundering, and farm labor. (Nevada Historical Society, eth00734.)

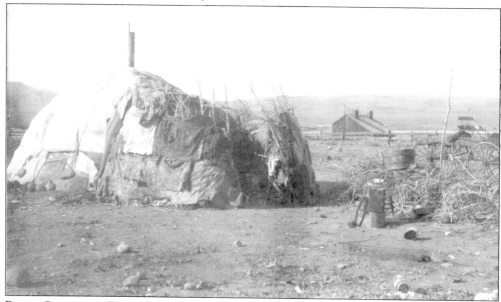

PAIUTE CAMPOODIE. Described as a Paiute *campoodie*, or camp, this *kani* was near Wadsworth in the early 1900s. The family used what was available in their environment to make their houses. That included cloth, possibly from the white settlers. The small structure off to the side may have been for cooking. Winter camps were located near the Truckee River and around Pyramid Lake with two or three related families living near each other. (Nevada Historical Society, eth00719.)

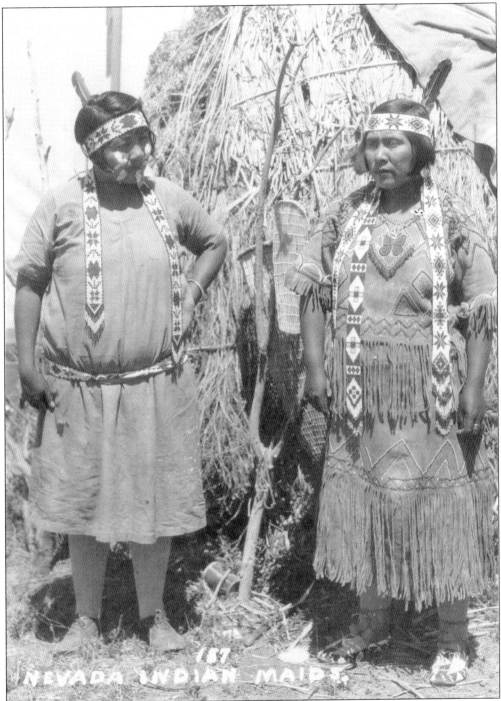

INDIAN MAIDS. Posing for a postcard are two Paiute women in traditional dress. Their calf-length dresses made of bighorn sheep or antelope skin had elbow-length sleeves. Fringe on the skirts was decorated with bone, shell beads, and porcupine quills. Headbands were made of buckskin, rabbit, or duck skin decorated with beads. The face painting usually worn for dancing was red, black, yellow, or white. (Nevada Historical Society, eth00373.)

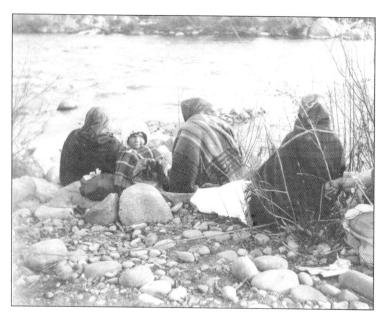

WASHING CLOTHES. Paiute women are washing clothes in the Truckee River near Reno in 1910. When living near white settlements and towns, traditional clothing changed to long cotton dresses, blankets, and scarves for women. Scarves rather than the traditional basket cap were worn to protect the women from the sun and wind. (Nevada Historical Society, eth00762.)

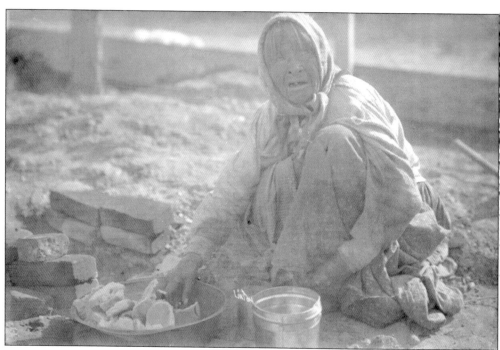

PREPARING A MEAL. A Paiute woman is shown preparing a meal near Wadsworth in 1905. The diet of the Northern Nevada Paiutes near Pyramid Lake was cui-ui fish, pine nuts, and sunflower seeds ground into flour to make mush or gruel. The pulp of chokecherries was made into small cakes that were dried and stored for later meals. (Nevada Historical Society, eth00778.)

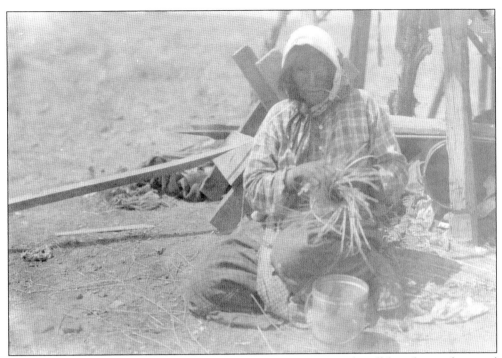

BASKET WEAVING. Winnowing baskets, burden baskets, water jugs, and cradleboards were decorated with black, red, and brown colors. Winnowing baskets, often made of tule, had black decoration from hair fern root. Water baskets, sealed with pitch, were cone shaped and flat-bottomed and made from willow, with leather or horse hair woven into the basket for handles. (Nevada Historical Society, eth00738.)

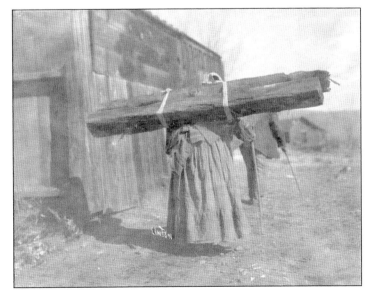

CARRYING WOOD. Paiute women like the one shown here carried firewood to their camps. This woman is carrying railroad ties in Wadsworth in 1905. The woman's husband is walking in front. Childcare and gathering activities were women's responsibilities. This photograph was taken by well-known Nevada photographer Esther L. Linton. (Nevada Historical Society, eth00753.)

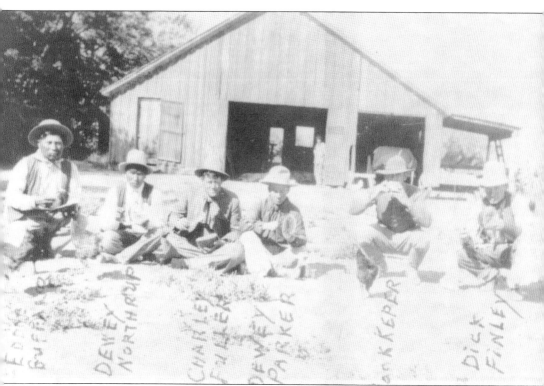

BUCKAROOS. Paiute and white buckaroos worked together at the Big Canyon Ranch near the Pyramid Lake Indian Reservation and the Dewey Parker Ranch near Gerlach in the 1910s and 1920s. Paiute cowboys worked at area ranches to help harvest hay and to move cattle between winter and summer ranges. Paiute cowboys also worked small herds of cattle on the reservation in the 1900s. Beginning in the 1870s, cattle from the northern Washoe County ranches may have been moved to winter pastures in the Truckee Meadows. Farmers advertised that they could feed and pasture cattle at a price per animal. A cattle drive brought the herd to Reno, or the herd was loaded into railway boxcars to go to Reno area ranches for the winter. After the cattle had wintered in Reno, they were shipped by train to markets in California. In the summer, cattle were pastured on railroad land or federal land. (Nevada Historical Society, wa06574.)

CHIEF WINNEMUCCA. Old Chief Winnemucca, son of Chief Truckee, led the Paiute tribe during the gold and silver rushes in California and Nevada when many white settlers first came to the area. Shown here in an army uniform, Chief Winnemucca had a pierced nose that had a stick of wood or bone through it. According to Ruth Hermann in *The Paiutes of Pyramid Lake*, Chief Winnemucca often wore a headdress of "otter or beaver skin, with magpie, eagle, or pelican feathers stuck into it." Old Chief Winnemucca died in October 1882 at age 82. (Nevada Historical Society, eth00063.)

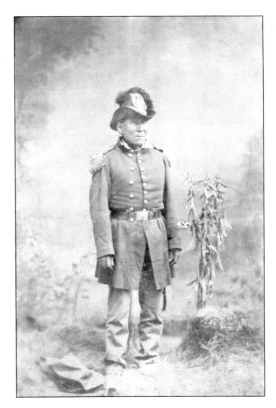

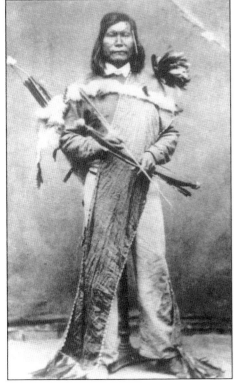

NUMAGA. Son of Old Chief Winnemucca and brother of Sarah Winnemucca, Numaga is shown here in traditional hunting gear. Numaga, chief of the Pyramid Lake Paiutes, led his tribesmen in the Pyramid Lake Indian War in 1860. Numaga died of tuberculosis on November 5, 1871, near Wadsworth. (Nevada Historical Society, eth00059.)

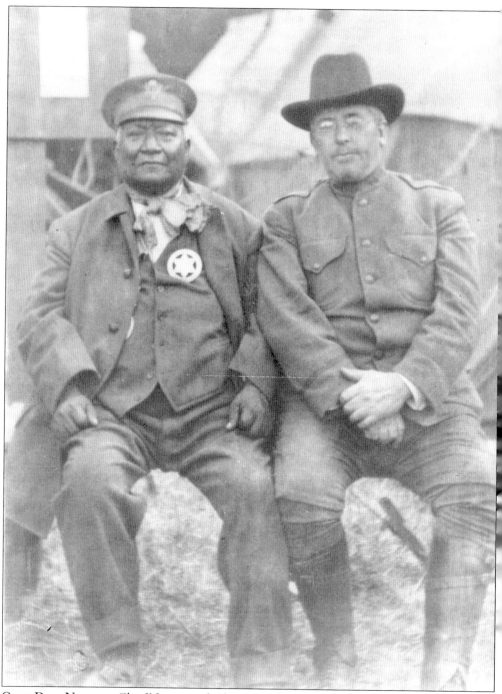

Chief Dave Numana. Chief Numana, also known as Captain Dave, was chief of police and chief justice of the court on the Pyramid Lake Indian Reservation. Captain Dave, cousin of Sarah Winnemucca, became chief after the death of Numaga in 1871. The United States Department of Indian Affairs presented a medal to Captain Dave in 1888 for his "meritorious services as a peace officer." Captain Dave is shown here with G.W. Ingalls, an Indian agent for Southern Nevada who traveled with John Wesley Powell in 1873. (Nevada Historical Society, eth00027.)

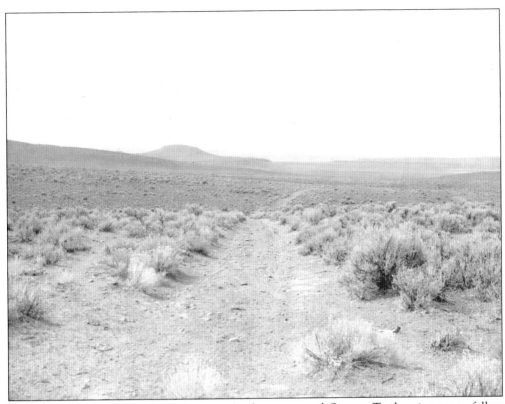

APPLEGATE-LASSEN TRAIL. In 1846, Jesse Applegate wanted Oregon Trail emigrants to follow his cutoff along the Humboldt River to California. In 1849, Peter Lassen built a trading post for emigrants using the Applegate-Lassen Cutoff. The cutoff went through the Black Rock Desert to Soldier Meadows through High Rock Canyon to Forty-Nine Pass and into Surprise Valley, California. In 1849, between 7,000 and 9,000 emigrants took this route. The extreme distance between water holes and marauding Indians made the route difficult. In the 1860s, miners and prospectors took the trail when going from California to the gold finds in Idaho. (Nevada Historical Society, trails00003.)

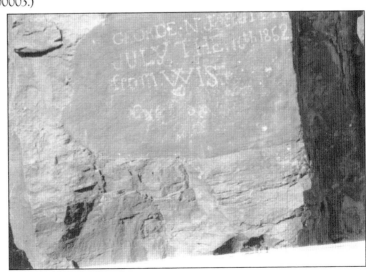

EARLY EMIGRANT. Graffiti etched on Register Rock in High Rock Canyon in northern Washoe County shows that George N. Jackson was passing through on the Applegate-Lassen Trail on July 16, 1852, from Wisconsin. (Nevada Historical Society, wa04858.)

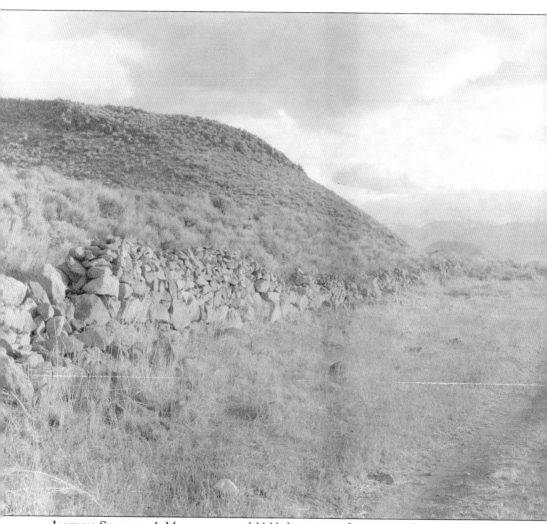

JAMISON STATION. A Mormon named H.H. Jamison or Jameson is thought to have been the first to set up a trading post in Washoe County in the fall of 1852. The rock wall shown here in the 1960s is thought to be the remains of the trading post. Jamison, who was living in Washoe Valley, drove a herd of cattle to a spot near where Steamboat Creek enters the Truckee River to build his trading post. Jamison bought thin, emaciated cattle from the emigrants who stopped at his trading post, fattened up the cattle, and then sold them to later emigrants on their way to California. Although the location is uncertain, the trading post is thought to have been in the Lower Truckee Canyon about three miles southeast of Sparks near what was to become Glendale. A few years later, John Stone and Charles Gates erected a ferry to cross the Truckee River and started a trading post west of Jamison's. (Nevada Historical Society, trails00048.)

Two

A Fertile Valley

A series of articles in the Weekly Gazette Stockman in September and October 1897 titled "A Fertile Valley" proclaimed, "If the hungry world knew what Nevada can produce she would be sending representatives here." Agriculture was important in the Truckee Meadows and all of Washoe County during the late 1800s until the1940s. Every early settler had a garden or orchard. In 1874, the Nevada surveyor-general said, "Whether he comes from the land of the orange or the apple, the first thing after building a shelter, the farmer sets out an orchard." By 1876, hay and potatoes were the most important crops in the county. In 1900, there were 331 farms in Washoe County, and there were 566 by 1925. Cattle and sheep ranches prospered in northern Washoe County, with its high mountain ranges and remote valleys. Dairy cattle, chickens, hogs, and horses were raised in the more fertile parts of the county. Most farms had beehives for honey. Alfalfa, hay, onions, cabbages, hops, and potatoes became the main crops. Apple, pear, and cherry orchards were planted along the sides of the mountains in an area termed the "thermal belt" in Washoe Valley. Air was warmer here than in the lower valleys, allowing the trees to survive cold nights. Agricultural products were shipped to miners in California and Virginia City and sold to emigrants passing through the county and to the newly arrived settlers. Cattle and sheep were brought from California to winter in the pastures of the Truckee Meadows. The article "Nevada's Agricultural Industry" in the September-December 1939 Nevada Highways and Parks stated that agriculture was "one of the largest tax-paying industries in the state."

Dude ranches, or divorce ranches, began in the late 1920s to provide comfort to those seeking a quick Nevada divorce. The first dude ranch opened in Washoe County near Pyramid Lake in 1926 and other ranches followed in Reno, Verdi, and Washoe Valley. These ranches expanded in 1931 after the residency requirements were reduced from three months to six weeks by the Nevada legislature. Guests took part in hunting, fishing, shooting, boating, swimming, skiing, and horseback riding during their required stay.

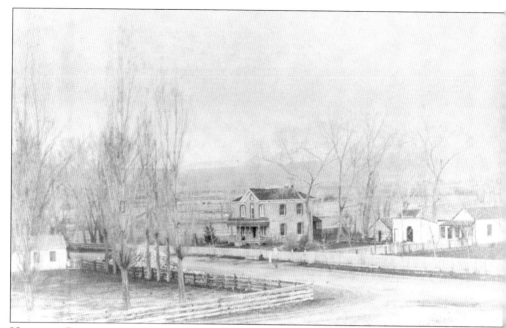

HUFFAKER RANCH. Granville Huffaker arrived in Washoe County in 1858 or 1859 with 500 head of cattle that he brought from Salt Lake City. Huffaker homesteaded his ranch south of Reno, establishing a trading post for emigrants going on to California. After his death in 1892, nephew Daniel Huffaker acquired the ranch. By 1897, the ranch, considered one of the best farms in the Truckee Meadows, had several acres in alfalfa with an apple orchard. (Nevada Historical Society, wa05226.)

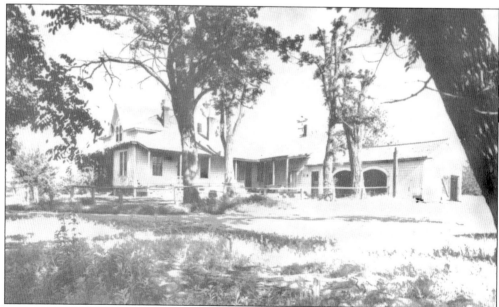

EDWIN FERRIS RANCH. Edwin Ferris, elected Washoe County commissioner in 1906, owned the ranch that was located at the corner of Hunter Lake and Mayberry Drive. At his death in 1916, the cattle ranches owned by Ferris in California's Plumas and Lassen Counties and Washoe County were worth $71,000. (Nevada Historical Society, wa00498.)

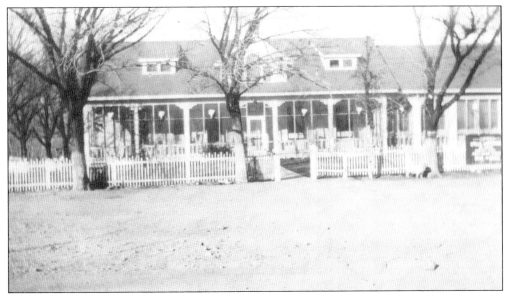

MAYBERRY RANCH. The Mayberry ranch, known as old Hunter's Station, was bought by James Mayberry in 1872. Mayberry came to Virginia City in 1862 as a wagon maker and had a planing mill in Verdi in 1868. Mayberry's mill made the doors and finishing trim for the Nevada State Capitol. Water to irrigate the ranch came from Hunter Creek and Last Chance Ditch. (Nevada Historical Society, wa02481.)

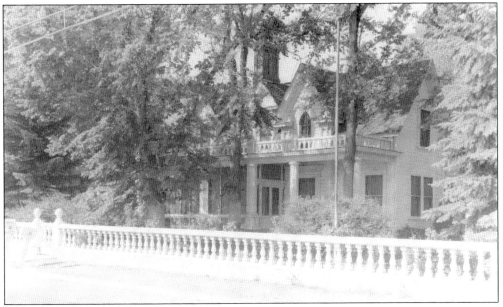

ALAMO HEREFORD STOCK FARM. The Alamo Ranch, located at what is now the corner of Peckham Lane and Virginia Street, was owned by John Sparks, governor of Nevada from 1903 to 1908. John Sparks and his wife, Nancy Elnora, brought southern hospitality to the Truckee Meadows hosting elaborate barbecues at the ranch. Hot water for each room in the ranch house and a 16-foot plunge bath came from two artesian geothermal wells. W.H. Moffat bought the ranch after the death of Governor Sparks, and in 1978 the house was moved to Pleasant Valley. (Nevada Historical Society, wa02488.)

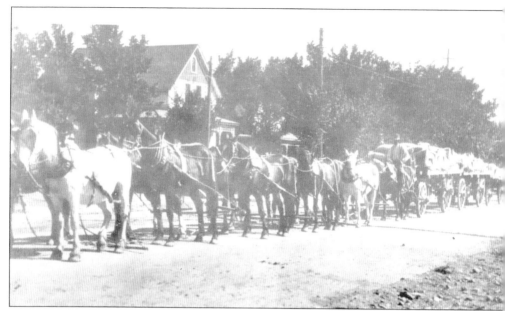

FARRETTO RANCH. This ranch, located in Steamboat Springs in south Truckee Meadows, was owned by Angelo Farretto. Alfalfa and wheat were grown on 230 acres, along with an apple orchard of 75 trees. With 10 dairy cows, the ranch produced 175 pounds of butter in 1897 that was sold in the Reno area. This mule-drawn wagon was carrying alfalfa to market in Reno. (Nevada Historical Society, wa00556.)

SHIPPING BILL. Agricultural products were shipped from the Truckee Meadows to Virginia City on the Virginia & Truckee Railroad. In 1912, wheat was shipped from the Lakeview Station in Washoe Valley to the Virginia City Station by Antonio Raffetto. Raffetto, in partnership with the Lagomarsino Ranch, often shipped produce to Virginia City. (Dan Webster collection.)

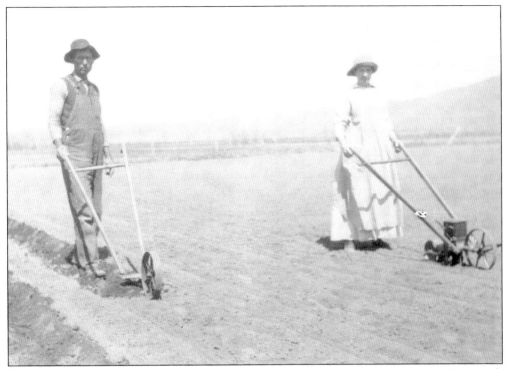

KLEPPE RANCH. John Kleppe and wife, Pearl, are shown spring seeding in 1899 on their ranch in Glendale. The Kleppe Ranch grew potatoes, onions, and alfalfa. Alfalfa seed was probably introduced in Washoe County in 1868 to replace native grasses for animal feed. An article in the *Reno Crescent* in 1872 told of ranchers seeding "sagebrush land in alfalfa" to make what was considered useless land into paying cropland. (Nevada Historical Society, wa06556.)

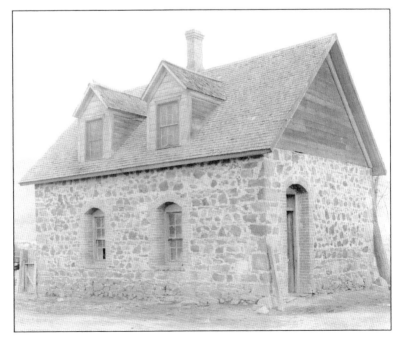

JONES DAIRY RANCH. An early dairy ranch in Glendale, the Jones Ranch shipped butter to Virginia City. The milk house in this photograph was described as being "cool as a cucumber" in an article in the *Weekly Gazette Stockman* in 1897. (Nevada Historical Society, wa00531.)

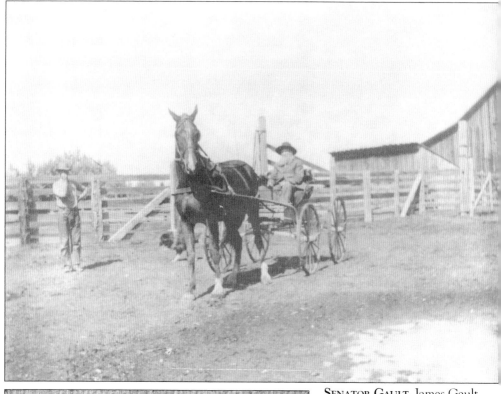

SENATOR GAULT. James Gault is in the buggy on the Jane and Charles Jones Ranch in 1900. James Gault, a well-known Glendale rancher, served as a Nevada state senator from Washoe County from 1912 to 1916. (Nevada Historical Society, wa05511.)

Who Was in Reno in 1870?

Fifty years ago James Gault settled in Washoe County.

For fifty years Mr. Gault has been identified with the upbuilding of Washoe County; has studied its needs and detected its mistakes. Mr. Gault is a candidate for the nomination for long-term.

Commissioner
on the Republican Ticket

For half a century Mr. Gault has demonstrated his business ability so that today he is recognized as one of the staunch citizens of the state. He is the owner of a 500-acre ranch located 5 miles N. E. of Reno; has raised a family and is in a position to devote his entire time to the office of commissioner from his district.

In 1912 Mr. Gault served this county as senator at Carson City.

He is an advocate of good roads, but insists that the money be spent wisely.

Your vote will not be lost if cast for James Gault.

PRIMARY ELECTION TUESDAY, SEPTEMBER 7.
(By Friends of the Candidate.)

JAMES GAULT FOR COMMISSIONER. James Gault ran for Washoe County commissioner in 1920. Gault had lived in Washoe County since 1870 and ran as an "advocate of good roads" with money spent "wisely." (Nevada State Library and Archives.)

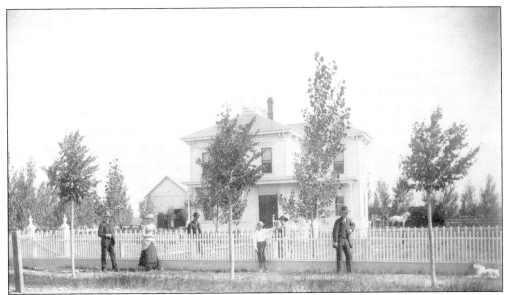

GOULD RANCH. The Gould Ranch, first operated by W.H. Gould, was a commercial creamery in the Truckee Meadows. The Reno Creamery was started by W.H. Gould's three sons after his death. Dairy products from many of the ranches in the area were collected by the creamery for production. The ranch was located east of the Virginia Street Bridge near Gould and Mill Streets. (Nevada Historical Society, wa02433.)

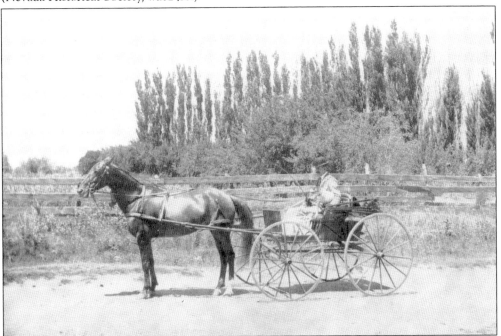

ALT RANCH. Located in Glendale, the Alt Ranch was known for its cabbage and onion crops. George Alt owned one of the most prosperous ranches in the Truckee Meadows. In 1885, Alt planted four tobacco stalks at the ranch, saying that he hoped that "good tobacco can be produced." Alt was an assemblyman from Washoe County from 1874 to 1876 and from 1886 to 1888. (Nevada Historical Society, wa00085.)

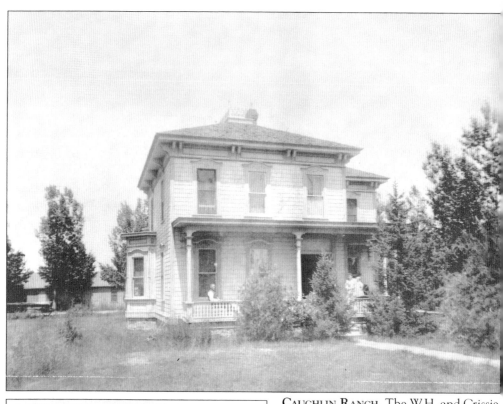

CAUGHLIN RANCH. The W.H. and Crissie Caughlin Ranch was one of the oldest ranches in the area, known as the old Andrews Ranch. It was located on the road to Verdi. By 1897, alfalfa, potatoes, and other vegetables were planted in 3,070 acres. Dairy cows produced butter and milk that were sold in Verdi and Reno. The ranch had an orchard of about 100 apple trees and 100 beehives. (Nevada Historical Society, wa05469.)

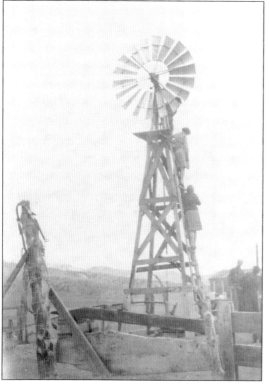

YOUNG RANCH. Windmills were used to pump water from wells for farm irrigation. Shown here is the Young Ranch that was in Palomino Valley north of Reno in 1927. (Nevada Historical Society, wa06563.)

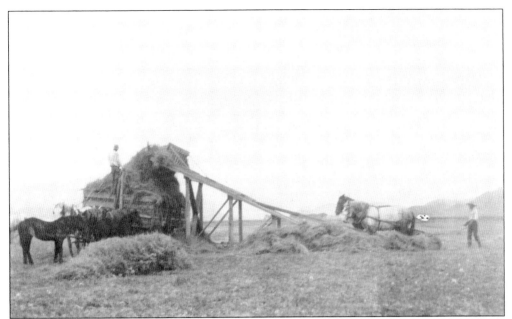

MATLEY RANCH. Hay was stacked using a horse-drawn derrick at the Matley Ranch in 1928. The ranch was located at the present Reno International Airport. Alfalfa and hay grew well in the dry, gravely soil, producing three cuttings and five tons per acre (Nevada Historical Society, wa06568.)

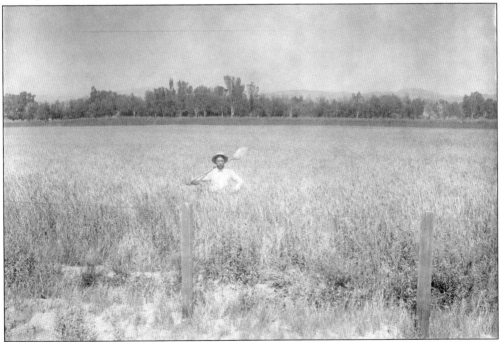

PECKHAM RANCH. Art Peckham, son of George E. Peckham, is shown here irrigating his alfalfa crop at the Peckham Ranch in the early 1900s. Hay, grain, and potatoes were grown on the ranch. George Peckham, a well-known political figure, ran on the Populist ticket for governor in 1894. (Nevada Historical Society, bio-p256.)

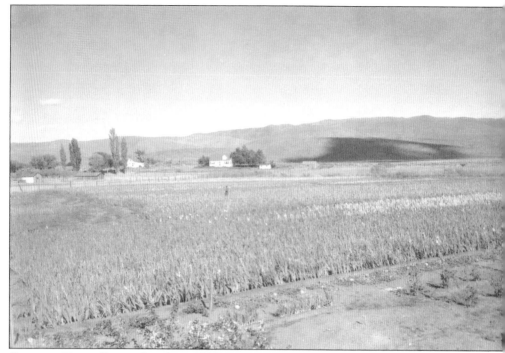

GLADIOLA FARM. Crops other than alfalfa were grown in Washoe County, shown by this gladiola farm that was located on South Virginia Street and Holcomb Lane in the 1940s and 1950s. A *Nevada State Journal* article in April 1955 described the gladiola fields as "bright colors dramatic against the hills." (Nevada Historical Society, wa04433.)

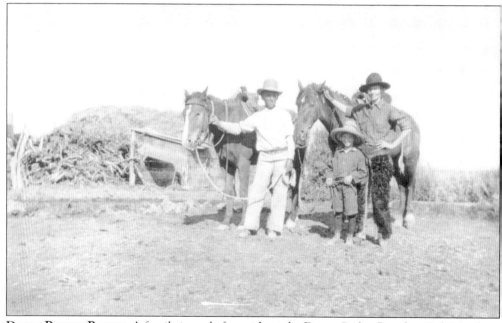

DEWEY PARKER RANCH. A family is ready for a ride at the Dewey Parker Ranch at Salt Meadows in northern Washoe County in 1914. A sagebrush corral is in the background of the photograph. (Nevada Historical Society, wa06560.)

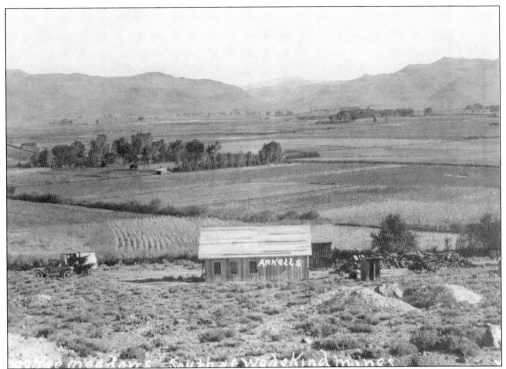

TRUCKEE MEADOWS. A panorama of the area south of Wedekind Mine in Sparks in the 1920s shows fields of alfalfa and hay being grown in the Truckee Meadows. Although not shown in this photograph, lavender and medicinal herbs were grown commercially at the San Antonio Ranch in Washoe Valley in the 1940s and 1950s. (Nevada Historical Society, wa00978.)

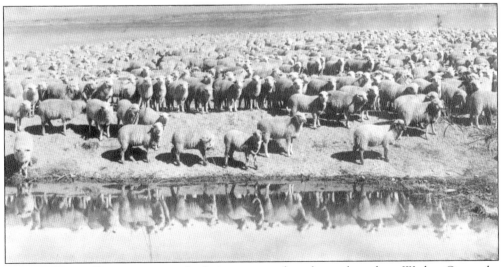

GRAZING SHEEP. Sheep, important for their mutton and wool, were brought to Washoe County by Daniel C. Wheeler in 1867. Wheeler purchased the sheep in Oregon, then drove them through the county to his ranch, which was near the location of the future Mapes Hotel. By 1900, there were 100,000 sheep in Washoe County. Here, sheep are grazing east of Sparks in 1910. (Nevada Historical Society, wa01001.)

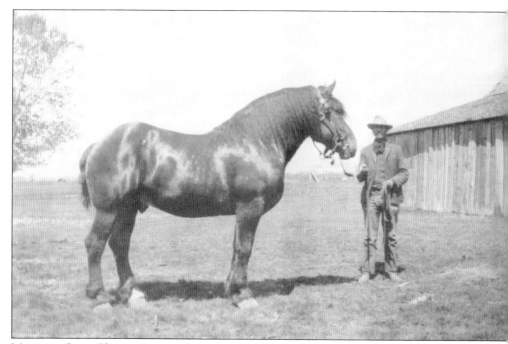

MORGAN STUD HORSE. An article in the *Reno Evening Gazette* in 1908 reported that Nevada was "fast making her mark as a producer of fast and swift horses." Horses bred and raised at an elevation of nearly 5,000 feet produced offspring with "broad chests, big lungs, and great powers of endurance." Shown here is John Kleppe with his Morgan horse. (Nevada Historical Society, wa06537.)

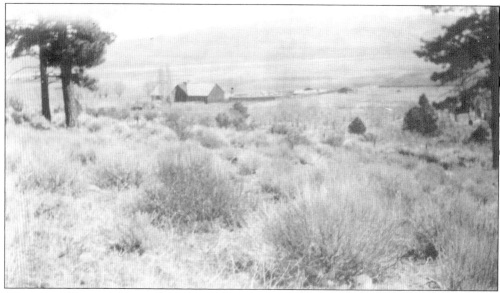

THEODORE WINTERS RANCH. Theodore Winters came to Washoe Valley with his brothers John D. and Joseph to run a contract freighting business to haul ore from Virginia City to Washoe City for milling. Theodore Winters became one of the largest landowners in Washoe Valley, with a ranch that included racehorses and a racetrack. Theodore Winters ran for governor as a Democrat in 1890 and 1894, losing in both races. (Nevada Historical Society, wa00476.)

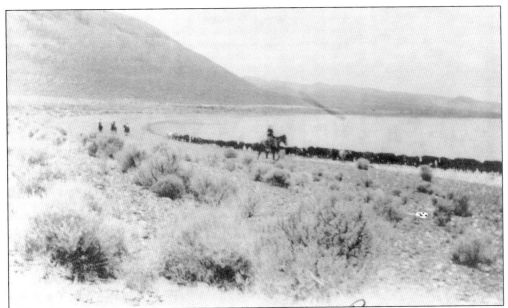

CATTLE AT PYRAMID LAKE. Cattle and sheep ranching were active in the late 19th century and early 20th century near Pyramid Lake and north to the Oregon border. Cattle in Nevada were usually Hereford or white-faced cattle. These cattle may have belonged to Patrick L. Flanigan. Flanigan had 5,000 cattle and 60,000 sheep on his ranches in Washoe County. (Nevada Historical Society, wa06620.)

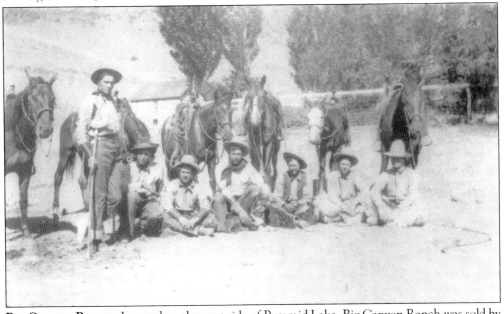

BIG CANYON RANCH. Located on the west side of Pyramid Lake, Big Canyon Ranch was sold by Mrs. Hannah Flanigan, widow of Patrick L. Flanigan, to Hiram D. West in 1925. West bought the ranch to raise livestock and renamed it The Circle S Ranch. The ranch became a dude ranch from 1934 to 1938 when owned by Beverly and Francesca Blackmer. Harry Richman, a songwriter, sportsman, and entertainer from New York, bought the ranch in 1949. (Nevada Historical Society, wa06557.)

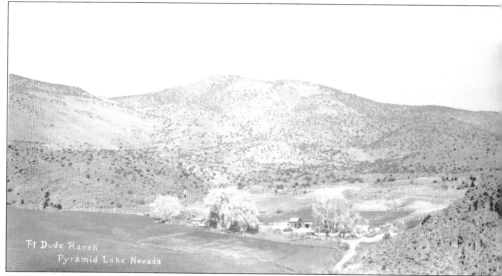

TH Dude Ranch. Patrick L. Flanigan owned the Hardscrabble Ranch, which was bought by Neill Hakes West in 1927. The ranch became one of the first dude ranches in Washoe County, known as the TH Dude Ranch, located near Pyramid Lake. Guests were met at the train station in Sutcliff in a wagon. (Nevada Historical Society, wa06640.)

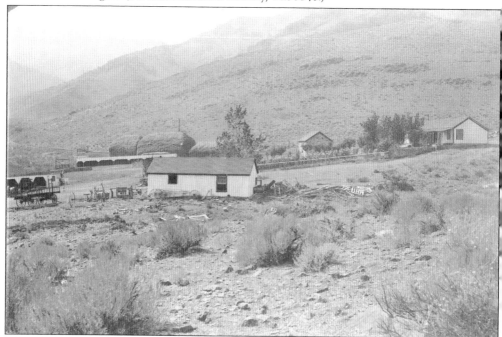

Flanigan Ranch. Patrick L. Flanigan owned 50,000 acres in northern Washoe County and California including the Hardscrabble Ranch, the Big Canyon Ranch, and the Smoke Creek Ranch. An article in the *Reno Evening Gazette* of August 13, 1954, stated that Flanigan was "the first to ship livestock in large quantities to eastern markets from this area." Flanigan, a state assemblyman from 1894 to 1896 and a state senator from 1896 to 1902, was a well-known Reno businessman who owned stock in Reno Power Light and Water Company and was part of the Flanigan Warehouse Company. The town of Flanigan, Nevada, was named for him. (Nevada Historical Society, wa00560.)

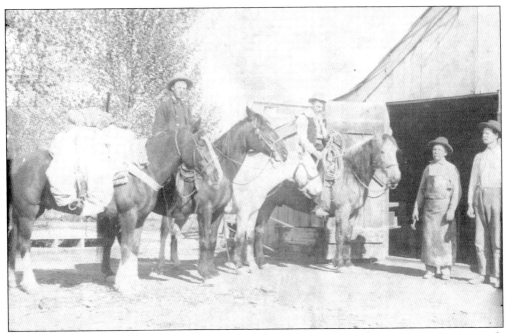

GERLACH CATTLE COMPANY. Cowboys are taking salt up to cattle in the mountain ranges north of Gerlach in 1890. M.E. Ward sold this ranch to Louis Gerlach in 1884. The ranch was expanded to about 2,000 square miles when sold in 1952 for $3 million, which was thought to be the largest ranch sale in western Nevada history. (Nevada Historical Society, wa00489.)

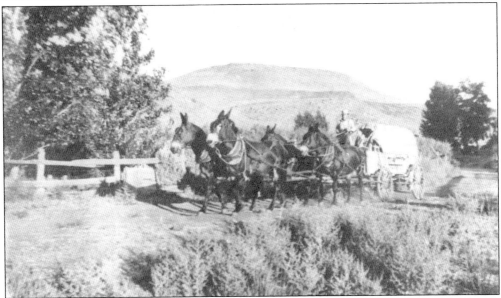

BUFFALO MEADOWS RANCH. A chuck wagon driven by the cook on the Buffalo Meadows Ranch in northern Washoe County was taking food and other supplies to cowboys in 1937. The chuck wagon was the center of life on secluded ranches. Cowboys came to the chuck wagon for medical supplies and tools and to get the orders from the superintendent. The *1902 Directory of Reno and Washoe County* said that mail was delivered by stage every Friday morning to Buffalo Meadows. (Nevada Historical Society, wa00558.)

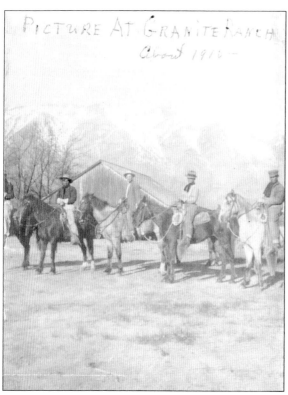

GRANITE CREEK RANCH. Buckaroos from the Granite Creek Ranch are saddled up to tend to their stock in the mountains in northern Washoe County. Paiutes were working as ranch hands in 1910 when the ranch was part of the Gerlach Cattle Company. In 1921, William McCarthy, owner of the ranch, was importing a Kentucky thoroughbred donkey "to raise for the market." (Nevada Historical Society, wa06577.)

WILLIAM DANA RANCH. Known as the Arrowhead D Ranch, this ranch near Pyramid Lake at Sutcliffe was well known for its award-winning horses, such as the one named Two-Step. The ranch was owned by William Shepherd Dana, publisher of the *Financial Chronicle* newspaper in New York City. (Nevada Historical Society, wa00526)

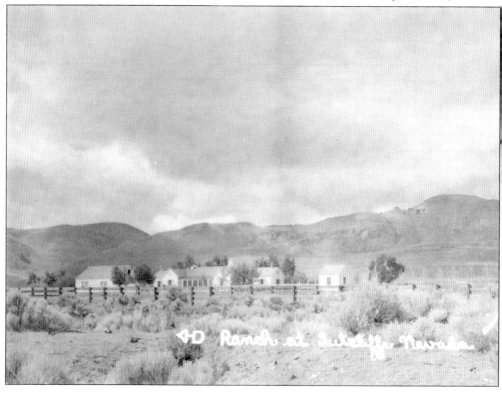

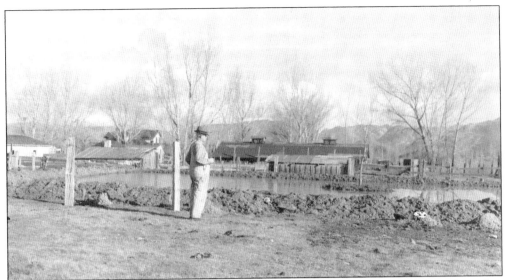

LONE STAR RANCH. In 1940, the Washoe County Farm Bureau recommended that all ranches build a water storage pond to use during ranch fires. The Lone Star Ranch had a pond that held at least 20,000 gallons of water and was 500 to 700 feet from farm buildings. (Nevada Historical Society, wa00543.)

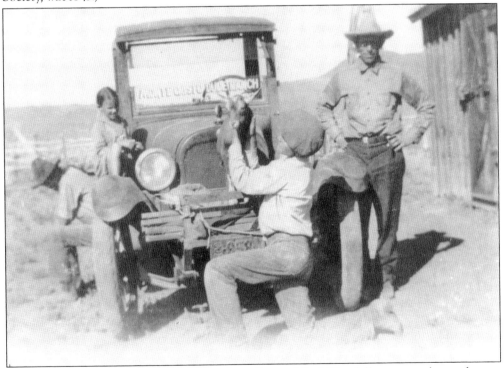

MONTE CRISTO DUDE RANCH CAR. Brothers Ike and Bud Blundell ran a cattle ranch near Pyramid Lake in 1899, changing it to a working dude ranch in the 1930s. It was advertised as "a real western cow ranch," and guests could ride horses, fish, and swim along with doing ranch chores. Ike (kneeling) is shown here with "Lige" (Henry Elijah) Langston, a well-known Nevada cowboy and rawhide braider (standing). (Nevada Historical Society, wa06549.)

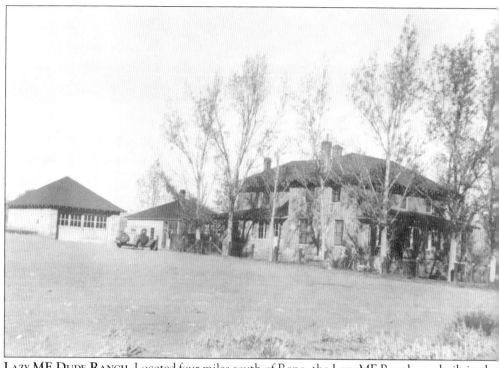

LAZY ME DUDE RANCH. Located four miles south of Reno, the Lazy ME Ranch was built in the 1920s by Cornelius Vanderbilt Jr. and Caleb Whitbeck. As a guest ranch, the Lazy ME offered steam heat and private baths. Amelia Earhart was invited to stay here when she flew her autogiro plane over the Sierra Nevada in June 1931. She missed the opportunity because bad weather forced her to land in Lovelock. (Nevada Historical Society, wa06635.)

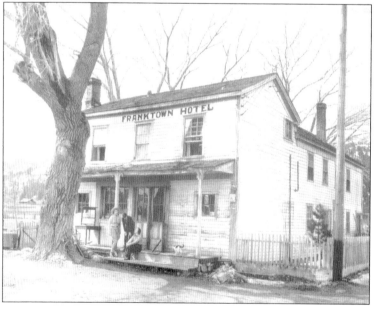

FRANKTOWN HOTEL. The Franktown Hotel or Railroad Hotel, built by George Seitz and Frederick A. Ent in 1861 or 1862, was located in Franktown on the corner of Fourth and Main Streets. Basil Woon called it the "hub of social life" for Franktown during the Comstock boom. The hotel property was said to be worth $5,000 in 1878. (Nevada Historical Society, wa00940.)

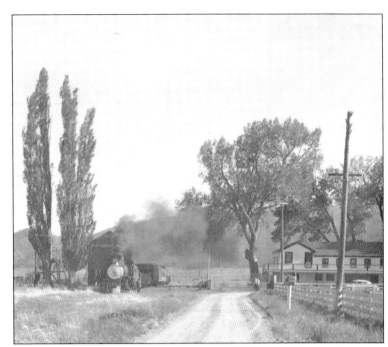

FLYING ME. The ranch that began as the Franktown Hotel was renovated by Emily and Dore Wood around 1938 to become the Flying ME Dude Ranch. Wood, in an article in the *Nevada State Journal* in 1956, described the Flying ME as "a bit of the Ritz dropped down in Nevada." The ranch was unfortunately destroyed by a fire in 1964. (Nevada Historical Society, rr00538.)

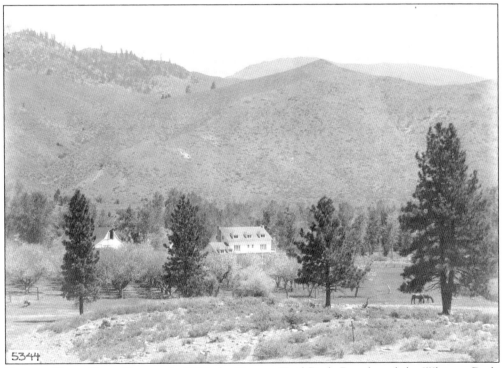

DONNER TRAIL DUDE RANCH. In 1969, the Donner Trail Dude Ranch and the Whitney Dude Ranch were the last two dude ranches in Washoe County. Located at the base of the mountains in Verdi, this 3,000-acre ranch was managed by Harry and Joan Drackert. The ranch had 22 rooms for guests, who paid $130 to $150 per week. Mary Rockefeller stayed here to establish her residency during her divorce from Nelson Rockefeller in 1962. (Nevada Historical Society, wa05344.)

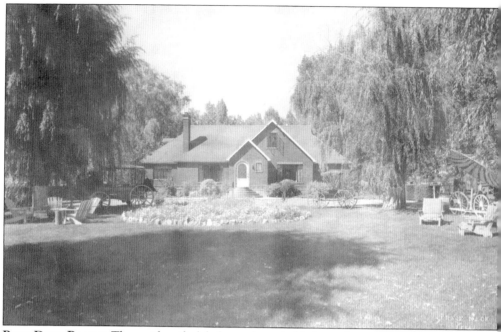

RENO DUDE RANCH. This unidentified dude ranch, probably located south of Reno, is an example of a divorce ranch during the heyday of dude ranches. Most divorce ranches had separate cabins or apartments with private baths. Ranches offered summer and winter rates with daily transportation to downtown Reno. The ranch owner or manager served as a witness in the divorce trial to state that the guest had been at the ranch every day for six weeks. (Nevada Historical Society, wa02553.)

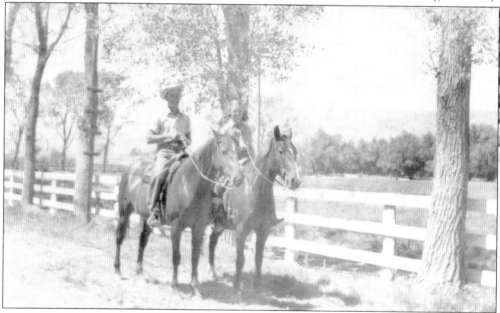

DOUBLE DIAMOND RANCH. Known for raising the best quarter horses in Nevada and a famous Aberdeen Angus bull named Dor-Mac, the Double Diamond Ranch was owned by Wilbur D. May and managed by H.M. "Rich" Richardson. Double Diamond Ranch was located south of Reno. The ranch had 1,500 head of cattle on 2,200 acres. (Nevada Historical Society, wa04373.)

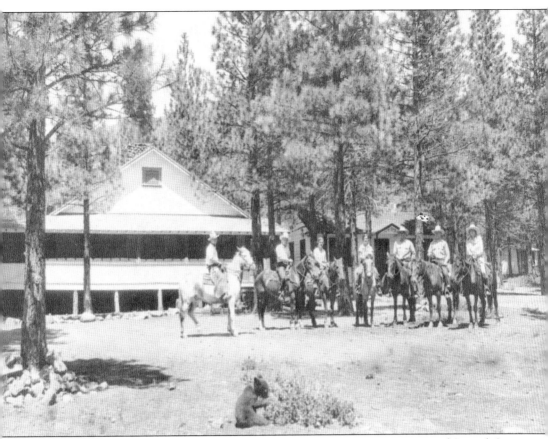

WASHOE PINES. Early owners of Washoe Pines included Charles Stout in 1914 and Daniel C. Wheeler in 1915. After Wheeler died in October 1915, Mrs. Amelia Wheeler took over ownership until selling the ranch to author and artist Will James and his wife, Alice, in 1923. Washoe Pines may have been the idea behind the movie version of the Clare Booth Luce play *The Women*. Enid Blackmer opened Washoe Pines as a dude ranch in 1936. The kitchen and living room were in the main ranch house and guests stayed in log cabins constructed around the ranch house. An advertisement in 1953 boasted of "winter sports in pine scented mountain air." Dr. Richard Miller and wife Maya Miller opened the Foresta Institute at Washoe Pines with a summer camp for children to study ecology in the 1960s and 1970s. (Nevada Historical Society, wa05004.)

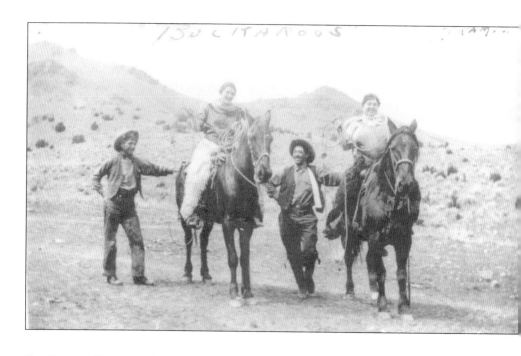

BIG CANYON RANCH. Above, buckaroos and guests are working at the Big Canyon Ranch in northern Washoe County in 1918. The women, attired in black and white woolly chaps, have their ropes ready to lasso cattle for branding. Beginning in 1873, brands were required to be registered with county recorders. In 1923, the Nevada State Board of Stock Commissioners began recording livestock brands, and the first brand book was published in 1924. Below, pack mules are ready to take ranch workers or guests out to the range at the Big Canyon Ranch in 1918. The woman, who has a gun in her right hand, is wearing white woolly chaps over a long skirt. (Above, Nevada Historical Society, wa6630; below, Nevada Historical Society, wa06618.)

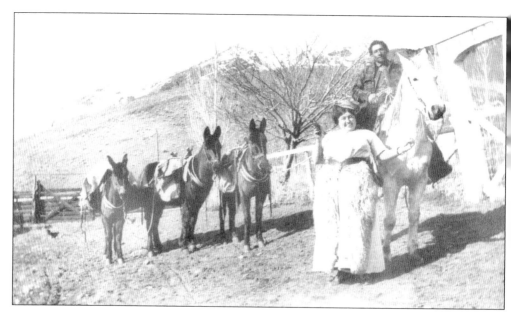

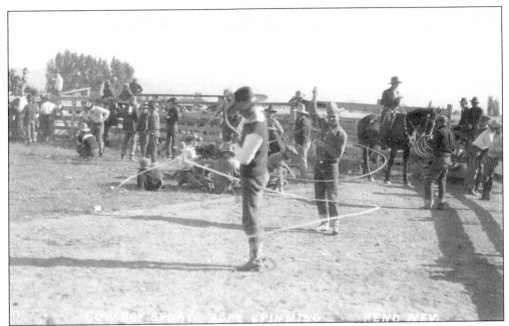

ROPE SPINNING. Cowboys would rope or lasso cattle on horseback, then jump off their horses to throw the cattle to the ground. Once secured on the ground, the cattle were branded, ear marked, and dehorned. Roping skill was demonstrated at local rodeos. (Southerland Studios.)

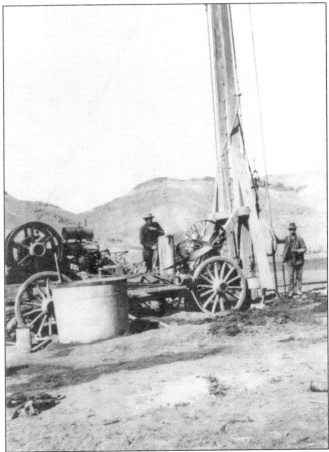

VOGEL AND WEISS RANCH ARTESIAN WELL. Ranches in Washoe County, and especially in northern Washoe County, often dug wells for irrigation. Artesian wells are defined by the Nevada Division of Water as "a well bored down to the point, usually at great depth, at which the water pressure is so great that the water is forced out at the surface." (Nevada Historical Society, wa06587.)

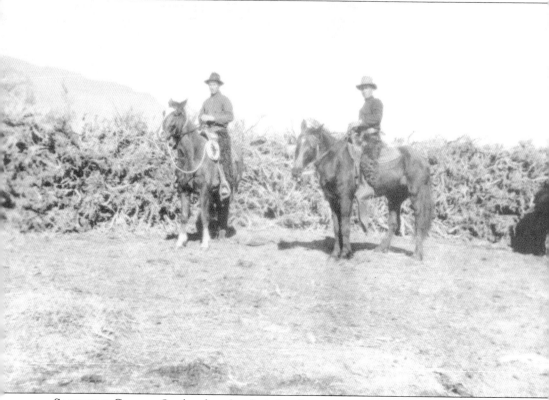

SAGEBRUSH CORRAL. Stacks of sagebrush tied with rope were used to form corrals like the one seen in this photograph in the 1920s at the Gerlach Cattle Company in northern Washoe County. Cattle, horses, and even antelope were driven into the corral. The opening on one side was then closed with more stacks of sagebrush. In 1909, there was a rush to find a use for the ubiquitous sagebrush. An article in the *Elko Daily Free Press* stated, "Every acre of the yellow blossoming plants that one sees is worth coin." There was hope that commercial rubber could be made from sagebrush. A young Reno inventor wanted to graft the California poppy onto sagebrush to produce a plant with golden leaves streaked with silver. Fields with sagebrush 8–10 feet high were considered good for growing other types of crops. The *artemisia tridentate* or *trifida* variety of sagebrush was made the official Nevada state flower in 1959. (Nevada Historical Society, wa06597.)

Three

RUSH TO WASHOE

The "Rush to Washoe" started before Washoe was a county with the discovery in 1859 of the Comstock Lode, a major silver and gold mining district on the east side of Mount Davidson in Storey County. Miners and prospectors rushed through Washoe County to reach the mines. Because there was water in Washoe Valley, quartz mills and sawmills were built in Ophir, Franktown, and Washoe City. Galena, 14 miles south of Reno, produced timber for the Comstock. Lumber and cordwood were used to build the mines and to provide fuel for power to crush the ore. Flumes were built in the Carson Range of the Sierra Nevada to bring the timber to the Washoe Valley mills. Oxen- or mule-drawn freight wagons loaded with lumber and supplies traveled to Virginia City. Wagons returned to Washoe Valley carrying ore for milling. Washoe County farmers and ranchers provided alfalfa and food to the Comstock mining camps. The Rush to Washoe lasted for almost 20 years. Washoe County grew from 571 in 1860 to 3,091 in 1870 and 5,664 in 1880. An article in the *Reno Evening Gazette* on October 28, 1915, reported, "Forty-five years ago the mountains southwest from Reno were a forest of pine—trees made many million of feet of sawn and hewed lumber, besides hundreds of thousands of cords of wood of the finest quality. The timber today is under Virginia City and helps that historical town to hang to the east side of old Mount Davidson and keep its upper stories in the clouds."

When the Comstock rush was over, prospectors and miners returned to Washoe County in search of gold, silver, lead, and copper. Prospectors always looking for the next big bonanza tried their luck in Jumbo, Olinghouse, Wedekind, and Poeville. An article in the September 2, 1897, *Weekly Gazette Stockman* said, "Take it all in all, Washoe county [sic] is likely to boom as no county in the State has boomed for twenty years."

However, mines in Washoe County proved not to be the next Comstock Lode.

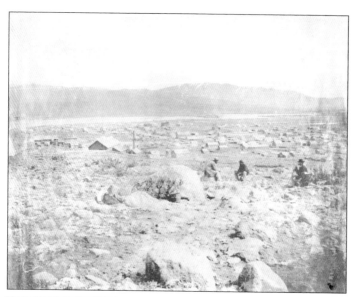

WASHOE CITY BIRDSEYE VIEW. Washoe City, located near Washoe Hill and Little Washoe Lake, was the site of the Atchison, New York, Buckeye, and Minnesota quartz mills and the Manhattan Reduction Works in the 1860s. As the largest town in Washoe County in the 1860s, Washoe City was the count seat from 1861 to 1871. Newspapers in Washoe City were the *Eastern Slope*, *Washoe Weekly Times*, *Washoe Weekly Star*, and *Old Pah Utah*. (Nevada Historical Society, wa00752.)

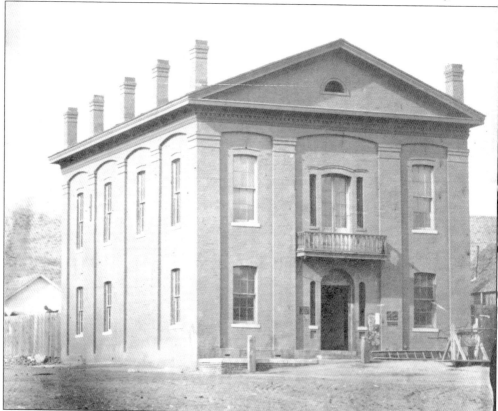

WASHOE CITY COURTHOUSE. John A. Steele was awarded the contract to build the Washoe City Courthouse for $15,000 in 1863. The contract to build the county jail was awarded on October 22, 1863, for $3,740. After Reno became the county seat in 1871, there was no need for a courthouse in Washoe City, and it was sold in 1873 for about $250. The brick from the building was taken to Carson City for the construction of a powder magazine. (Nevada Historical Society, wa00754.)

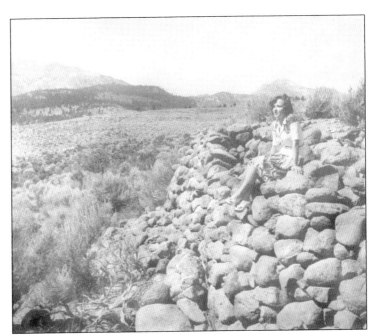

RUINS OF WASHOE CITY ORE MILL. When the county seat was transferred to Reno in 1871 and the Virginia & Truckee Railroad was completed from Carson City to Virginia City, Washoe City began its decline. Washoe City's population of 552 in 1870 declined to 91 in 1880. In July 1875, the *Nevada State Journal* stated, "once the liveliest camp in the state is now termed 'dead' and is almost entirely deserted." (Nevada Historical Society, wa00774.)

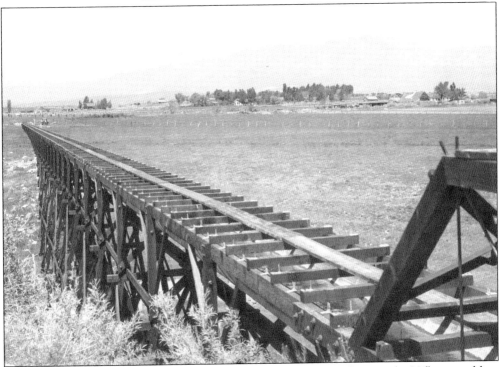

VERDI BOX FLUME. Two types of flumes built in the Sierra Nevada were the V-flume and box flume. A box flume, like the one shown here, was made of 2-inch-thick pine. V-flumes were made of planks that were 1.5–2 inches thick attached at right angles to form the "V," with an opening about 2.5 feet wide. Flumes, placed on trestles that could be as high as 70 feet, were filled with water to move logs from the Sierra Nevada Range to sawmills and to bring water for irrigation and power. (Nevada Historical Society, wa00660.)

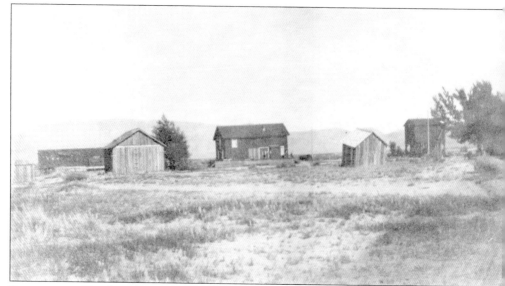

FRANKTOWN. Franktown was laid out by Mormon elder Orson Hyde in 1856 with 1.25-acre irrigated lots. Residents of Franktown were mostly farmers and sawmill workers. A wood flume built by the Virginia and Gold Hill Water Company ran from Little Valley to Franktown. The population was 271 in 1870 and 113 in 1880. (Nevada Historical Society, wa00945.)

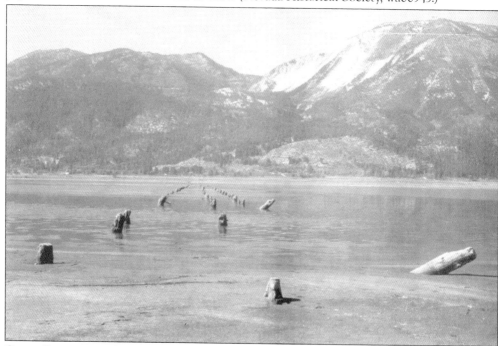

OPHIR CAUSEWAY. A bridge over Washoe Lake built by the Ophir Gold and Silver Mining and Milling Company was used to carry ore from mines in Virginia City down to the Ophir quartz mills. The Ophir Causeway was built for $75,000. Oxen teams or mule teams pulled freight wagons loaded with ore down the Ophir Grade and over the causeway. The Ophir Grade was thought to be the busiest road in the country during the Comstock days, with a continuous line of wagons. This photograph shows the remains of the causeway in 1976. (Nevada Historical Society, wa00786.)

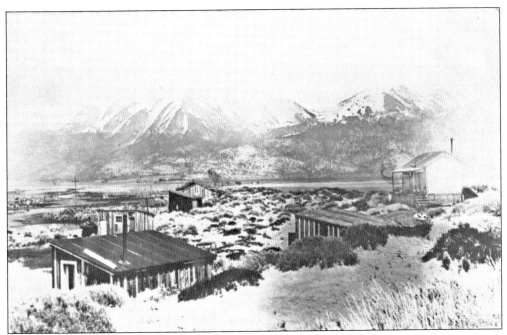

OPHIR MILL. Ophir was located in Washoe Valley three miles from Washoe City and one mile from Franktown. The Ophir Gold and Silver Mining and Milling Company of Virginia City set up its quartz mill and reduction works in Ophir. The quartz mill had 72 stamps and cost $500,000 to build. William L. Dall, superintendent of the mill, was paid $30,000 per year. (Nevada Historical Society, wa09872.)

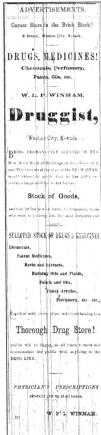

DRUGGIST. W.L.P. Winham, a druggist in Washoe City, advertised in the September 9, 1865, *Eastern Slope*. Winham gives the location of the store in the new "brick block" on E Street. Washoe City's commercial district was on E Street between First and Fifth Streets. Patent medicines, herbs and extracts, and burning oils and fluids were some of the items sold. (Nevada State Library and Archives.)

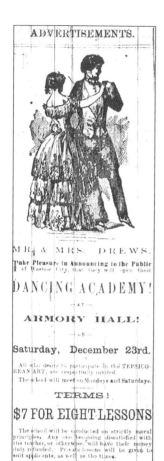

DANCE LESSONS. Dance lessons were offered by Mr. and Mrs. Drews at their Dancing Academy beginning in 1865. Grand balls were held to celebrate St. Patrick's Day, Washington's Birthday, the Fourth of July, and New Year's Eve. Balls began with a grand march at 8:00 p.m. and lasted late into the night. A midnight supper was often served. (Nevada State Library and Archives.)

JUMBO, 1920. Jumbo, often called West Comstock, was located on the west side of Mount Davidson. The first discovery at Jumbo was in 1859, but it was only an active mining site from 1861 to 1863. In 1908, Rolla Clapp said "I believe that Jumbo will be the biggest and best camp in the state before the summer is over." (Nevada Historical Society, wa00175.)

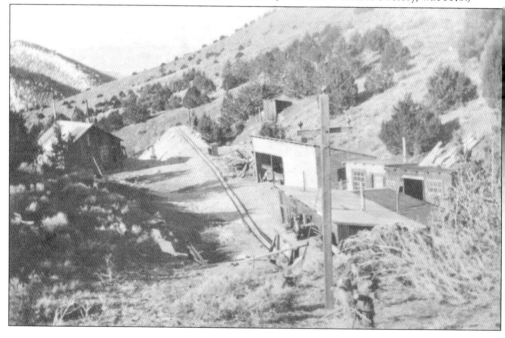

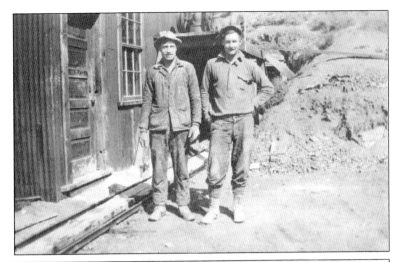

JUMBO MINERS. Two miners are preparing for work at the Jumbo mining camp in 1920. The original name of the Jumbo mining district was Argentine. Miners and prospectors were looking for gold, silver, and tungsten. (Nevada Historical Society, wa00172.)

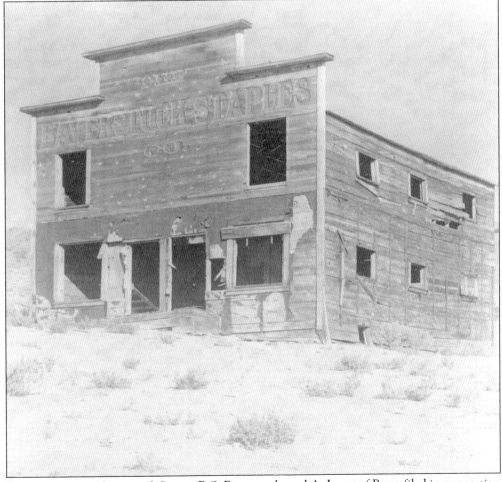

BAVORSTOCK AND STAPLES. J. Payne, R.S. Bavorstock, and A. Jarott of Reno filed incorporation papers on May 9, 1908, so they could open a general store and assay office in Jumbo. (Nevada Historical Society, wa00176.)

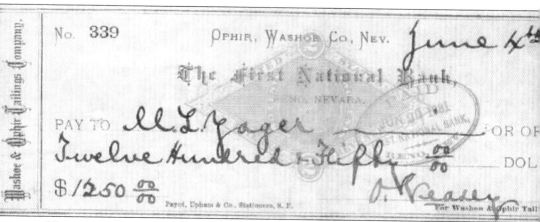

WASHOE AND OPHIR TAILINGS COMPANY. In July 1881, the Washoe and Ophir Tailings Company of Ophir, Nevada, shipped 7,512 ounces of bullion to San Francisco. The bullion was obtained from reworking the tailings from the mills that had processed the Comstock ore. The Washoe process, crushing the ore with stamps and then separating it in settling tanks and slurry, was used on the Comstock. The tailings were the small rocks and sand left over. The Washoe & Ophir Tailings Company reprocessed the tailings from the Atchison, New York, Buckeye, Minnesota, and Ophir quartz mills. Mill tailings from the Comstock mines were reprocessed until the 1920s. (Dan Webster collection.)

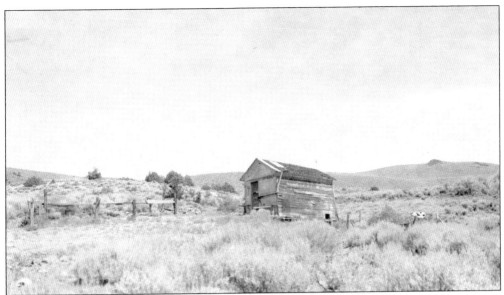

JUMBO RUINS, 1930. The Jumbo Post Office closed in November 1910, and by the 1930s mining at Jumbo had stopped. Miners and prospectors moved on and the buildings were left to deteriorate. (Nevada Historical Society, wa00170.)

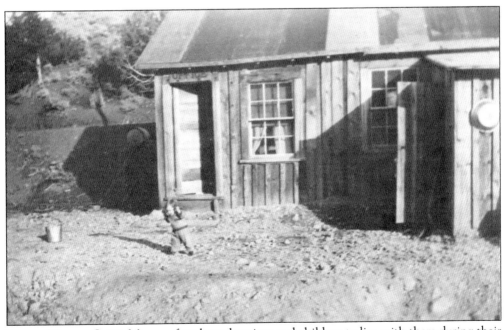

LIFE IN MINING CAMP. Miners often brought wives and children to live with them during their stay at mining camps. Shown here in 1920 is a young child playing in front of a cabin in Jumbo. (Nevada Historical Society, wa00174.)

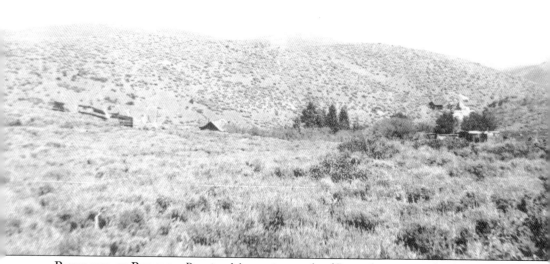

PANORAMA OF POEVILLE. Peavine Mountain, north of Reno, has two peaks that are over 8,200 feet in elevation. The area was an active mining site with a mining camp called Poeville, Poe City, Podunk, and Peavine from the 1860s until the 1920s. This photograph shows the remains of Poeville in 1952. Peavine was named for the wild peavines that grew near Peavine Springs. A poem by William Piedmont celebrating the beauty of Peavine Mountain in the 1932 *Nevada State Journal* begins with the following:

> Oh! Peavine old
> Its glory told
> By poets long since dead;
> It lingers on
> Like the Wild Bird's song
> As it sings in its lonely bed.

(Nevada Historical Society, wa00250.)

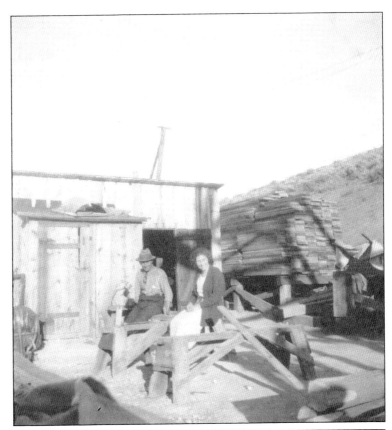

FRAVEL PAYMASTER MINE LUMBER YARD. The Paymaster Mine, one of the oldest mines on Peavine Mountain, was discovered by John Poe in 1874, then worked by Captain A.D. Griffin for 25 years from the late 1880s. At the time of this photograph in 1927, the Standard Metals Company was hoping to continue production. (Nevada Historical Society, wa00247.)

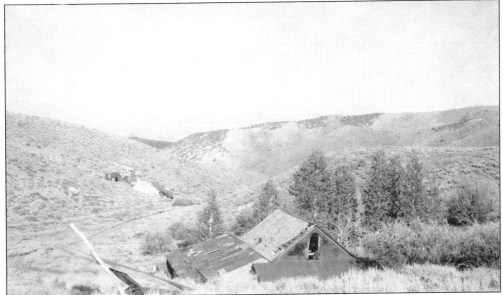

GUS NORDSTROM'S HOUSE. Miner and prospector Gus Nordstrom worked his Gold Bond Mine located above the Fravel Paymaster Mine on Peavine for 27 years. Nordstrom's obituary in February 1941 said that he had sunk a "165 foot shaft single handedly." The mine went into production in February 1942 for a short time. (Nevada Historical Society, wa00253.)

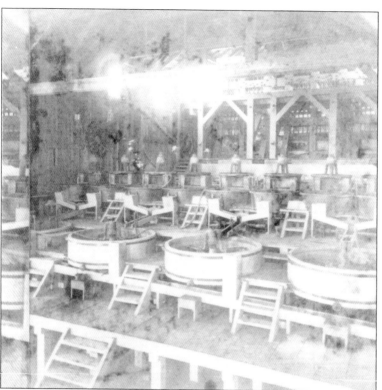

ENGLISH COMPANY QUARTZ MILL. Located in Auburn, an area northwest of Glendale, this quartz mill was built by the Washoe United Consolidated Gold and Silver Mining Company of London. In 1865, the English Mill Ditch produced the horsepower needed to run the mill. It was hoped that the English Mill Ditch would provide water for irrigation for 20,000 acres in Spanish Springs. (Nevada Historical Society, wa06353.)

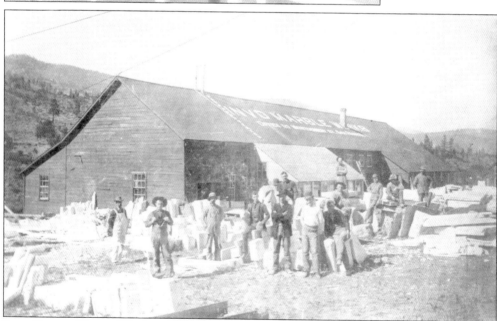

INYO MARBLE WORKS. The Inyo Marble Works, located at Marmol near Verdi, employed 15 to 20 men from 1890 until it closed in 1908. Marble was shipped from Inyo, California, on the Southern Pacific Railroad to Mound House, then transferred to the Virginia & Truckee Railroad to be transported to Marmol to be finished and polished. The Hobart building in San Francisco used polished marble from the Marmol plant. (Nevada Historical Society; wa04349.)

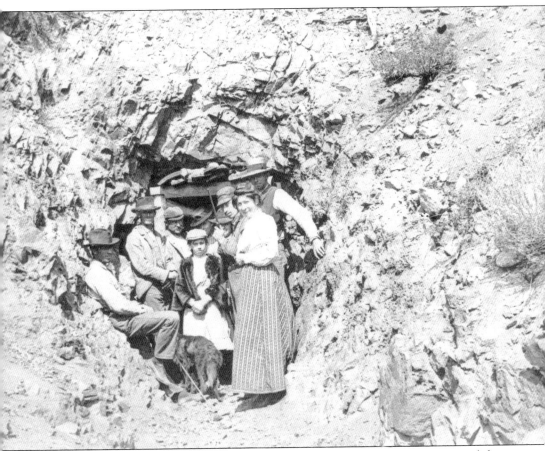

IMPERIAL MINE. A family living in Poeville (Peavine) is standing in front of a water tunnel that brought water from the Lemmon Ranch to Peavine in 1895. Mary Hogan, with husband John Hogan and daughter, are shown here. Poeville, a community on the east side of Peavine, had the Golden Eagle Hotel and a post office in 1874. A school was built in 1876. Poeville, named for John Poe, was also known as Podunk, Poe City, and Peavine. The Imperial Mine, part of the Golden Fleece Company along with the Poe and Paymaster mines, produced 29,579 tons of ore worth $148,464 from 1872 through 1876. Owners of the Imperial mine were Thomas K. Hymers, Marcus Lippman, and David Lachman. Stock certificates were sold for $10 per share. The mine closed in 1877 when the cost of mining was more than the gold or silver taken from the mine. (Nevada Historical Society, wa00255.)

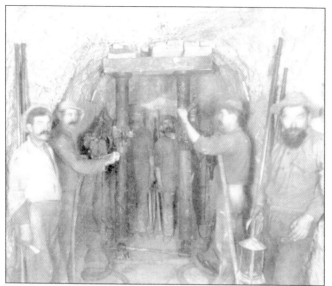

UNDERGROUND AT THE WEDEKIND MINE. Miners were working in underground tunnels at the Wedekind Mine as early as 1900. Underground mining was extremely hazardous, with miners subject to extreme heat, lack of ventilation, and in some mines, scalding water. Because of the heat, underground miners constantly consumed ice and ice water that caused cravings of highly salty food such as pickles and ham. The miners worked 8–10 hour shifts, getting paid from $3 to $5 per day. (Nevada Historical Society, wa00838.)

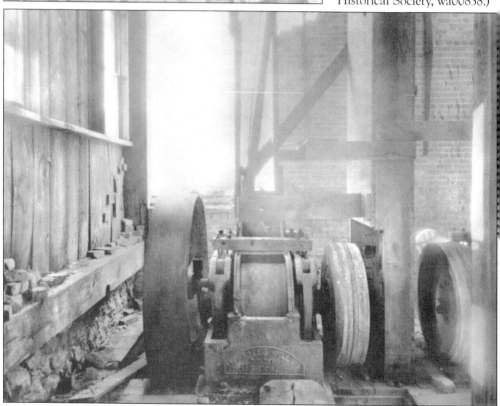

WEDEKIND MINE ROCK BREAKER. An article about the rock crusher at the Wedekind Mine in the September 10, 1902, *Nevada State Journal* reported, "The ore is conveyed by a track from the mine into the ore bins where it is carried to the rock-breaker and Merrall rolls. Then it is placed in a huge revolving Buckner roaster and chemically treated in tanks." The Merrall rock crusher had an output of 140 tons in 24 hours, producing crushed rock that would go through a six-mesh screen. (Nevada Historical Society, wa00830.)

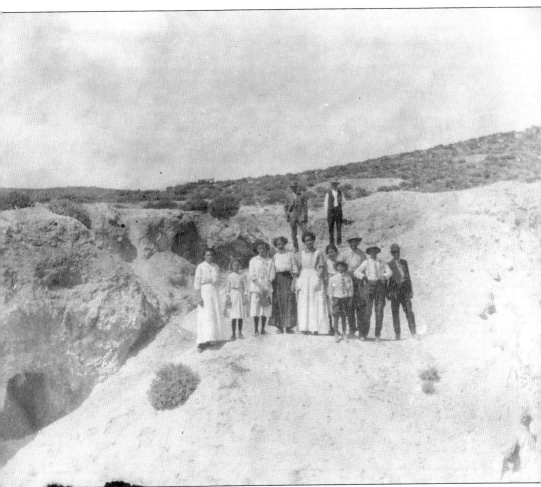

WEDEKIND MINE. Located two miles north of Sparks, the Wedekind mining camp was named for George Wedekind, who was the first to discover gold in the area. Wedekind, a piano tuner, shipped the first ore out of the Wedekind Mine in the early 1900s. John Sparks bought the property, making C.L. Crane superintendent and Will Bryant foreman. A barbecue to celebrate the change of ownership, held on September 10, 1902, prompted Mrs. H.H. (Christine) Clark to write a poem ending with the following:

> We bring to him a bar of silver bullion
> The first from out his mill—
> A true memento of this day of pleasure
> And may his coffers fill
> To overflowing as a final measure
> And in one voice is due
> These grand and glorious words
> Long live John Sparks
> He gave the barbecue.

(Nevada Historical Society, wa05513.)

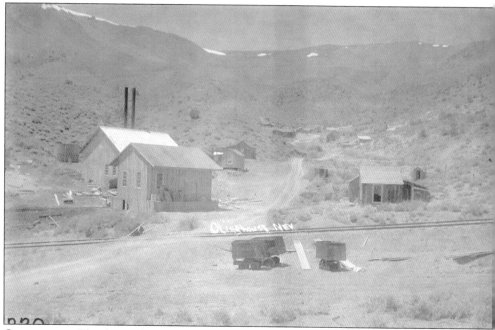

OLINGHOUSE. Olinghouse, located about six miles west of Wadsworth on the east side of the Pah Rah range, was named for rancher Elias Olinghouse. A railroad, built by the Nevada Consolidated Mining Company, connected the mines to stamp mills in Wadsworth. A celebration for the opening of the railroad line in May 1906 brought many people from Reno to Olinghouse for the festivities. By the end of 1906, the boom was over and the residents left. (Nevada Historical Society, wa00220.)

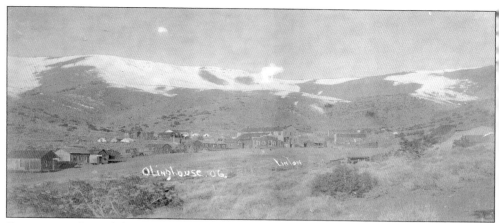

OLINGHOUSE. Part of the White Horse Mining District, Olinghouse was first prospected in the 1860s by Bill Williams. Gold was discovered in the late 1890s, leading miners to think Olinghouse would be the next big bonanza. In 1903, Olinghouse had cabins, bunkhouses, two windmills, and storage rooms for the newly arrived miners. The railroad was the shortest-lived railroad in Nevada, operating until 1907 and being dismantled in 1909. The Olinghouse jail was sold in 1931 for $10. (Nevada Historical Society, wa00221.)

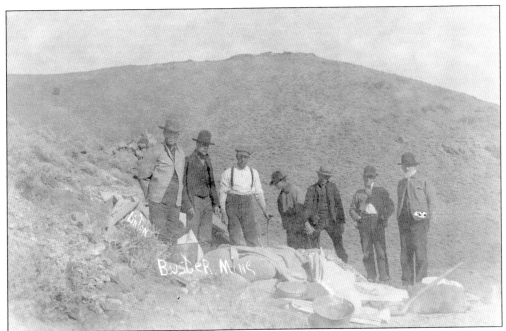

BUSTER MINE. Owned by Buck Ingalls, the Buster Mine Group in Olinghouse Canyon was the center of a lawsuit in 1905 brought by the Central Pacific Railroad to declare the property agricultural land rather than mineral land. Men were working at the mine in 1906 in this photograph. (Nevada Historical Society, wa00225.)

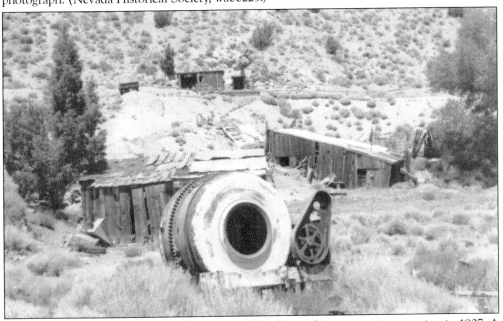

OLD RENEGADE MILL. The Renegade Mine in Olinghouse Canyon was in operation in 1907. A *Nevada State Journal* article on November 14, 1907, told about the rich discoveries: "a streak of pay ore a foot in width had opened up would average $200 to $300 per ton." A rich strike of ore was reported in the December 1907 *Pacific Miner*. A stamp mill opened in 1907. The remains of the stamp mill are shown in 1969. (Nevada Historical Society, wa00200.)

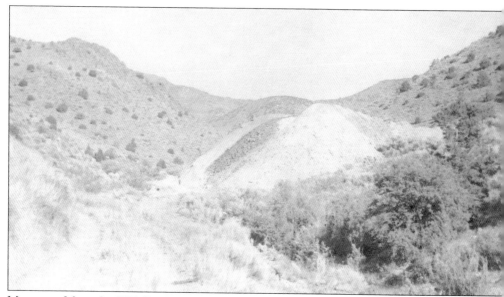

MONARCH MINE. In 1876, Dr. Simeon L. Bishop of Reno made a claim on 1,500 feet of gold and silver property near Pyramid Lake that he named Monarch. The mining camp became Pyramid City, located 26 miles northeast of Reno. A *Nevada State Journal* article on June 10, 1876, said that there was hope that the Pyramid Lake mines would become another Comstock Lode. Other mines in the area were the Red Rover, Pinto Chief, Gulch, and Pride of the Lake. (Nevada Historical Society, wa00179.)

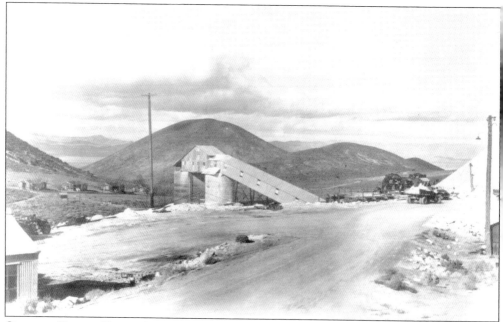

GERLACH GYPSUM PLANT. In 1924, the Pacific Portland Cement Company built a gypsum mill five miles from Gerlach in what was to become Empire. The Empire plant could produce 500 tons per day with a six-kettle plant and was claimed to be "the largest plaster mill west of the Rocky Mountains." The *Nevada State Journal* of May 4, 1924, stated that this gypsum was known throughout the world. (Nevada Historical Society, wa00184.)

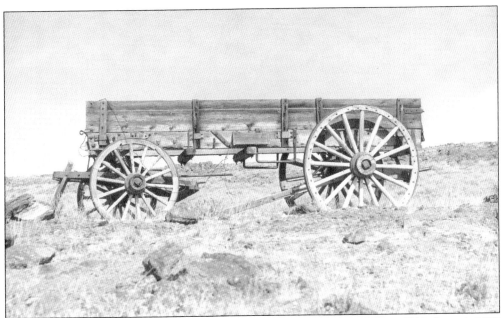

LEADVILLE ORE WAGON. The mining community of Leadville lasted from 1910 through 1927 with miners looking for lead and silver. Leadville is about 40 miles north of Gerlach. An article in *Desert Magazine* in June 1968 said that the Leading Mining Company operated the mine in 1920 with a "1700-foot tunnel with a 35-ton mill and flotation plant." (Nevada Historical Society, wa00092.)

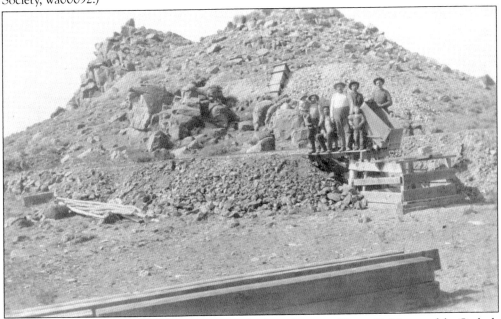

DONNELLY MOUNTAIN MINE. Discovered in 1902 by James Raser and James D. Murray of the Gerlach Cattle Company, the mine was located in the Granite Creek or Donnelly mining district on Division Peak in the Calico Mountains between Washoe and Humboldt Counties. Ore from the mine was on display at the Overland Hotel in Reno in 1906. The Donnelly Mountain Mine had a five-stamp mill in 1911 that produced $90,000 in gold bullion. (Nevada Historical Society, wa00492.)

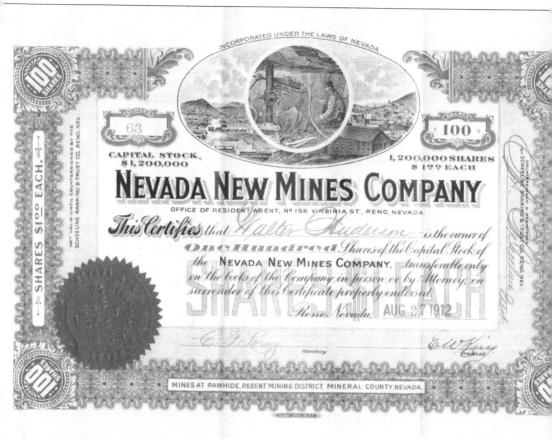

NEVADA NEW MINES COMPANY. Reno, the largest city in the state in the early 1900s, was the business center for mining companies. Companies would file corporation papers with the secretary of state in Carson City, then set up offices with their resident agents in Reno. The Nevada New Mines Company had mines in Rawhide, Regent Mining District, Mineral County, Nevada. The old American sayings "A mine is a hole in the ground with a liar at the top" and "A mine is a hole in the ground owned by liars" describe mining in Nevada at the time. Mining companies sold stock certificates to the public with very little information on the mine, hoping the investors were blindly looking for the next big bonanza. More often than not, the next bonanza never came and the investors lost all of their money. (Dan Webster collection.)

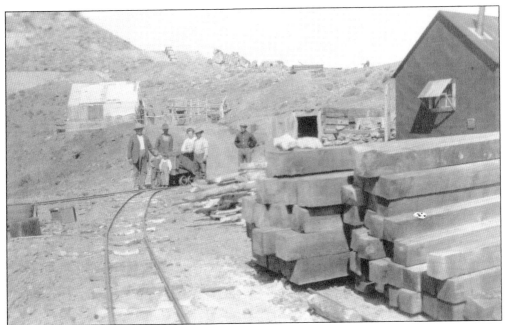

DONNELLY MOUNTAIN MINE, 1910. A legend often told about the Donnelly Mountain Mine is that an Indian would show large pieces of gold to miners saying that he would take them to the gold. Miners followed the Indian only to quickly lose track of him, never finding the gold. (Nevada Historical Society, wa06354.)

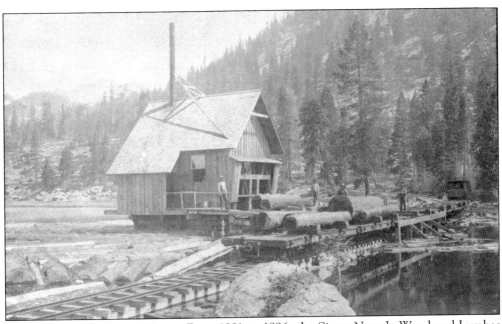

SAND HARBOR LOGGING TRAIN. From 1881 to 1896, the Sierra Nevada Wood and Lumber Company, one of the largest lumber companies in the Sierra Nevada, provided lumber from the Lake Tahoe Basin to the Virginia City mines. Logs were towed from the south end of Lake Tahoe by the steamer *Niagara* to Sand Harbor, where they were taken to the Mill Creek sawmill by rail, then flumed to Washoe Valley. (Nevada Historical Society, lt00447.)

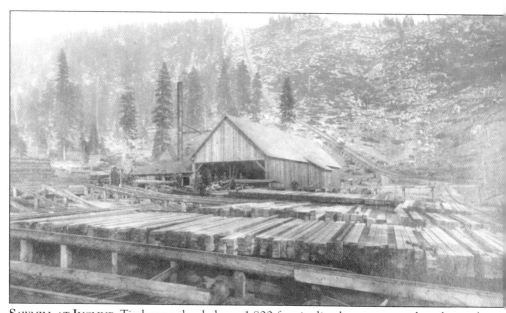

SAWMILL AT INCLINE. Timber was hauled up a 1,800-foot incline by a tramway, then dumped into a V-flume to descend to the mills in Washoe Valley. Wagons then took the wood to Virginia City. Incline (Village) was named for this steep incline. The Incline sawmill near Mill Creek was one mile east of present day Incline Village near Sand Harbor. The tramline can be seen to the right of the mill. (Nevada Historical Society, lum00044.)

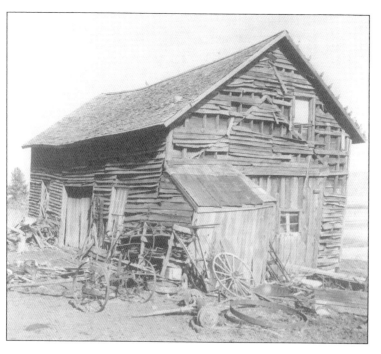

CLIFF RANCH BLACKSMITH SHOP. Lumber to build this blacksmith shop on the Cliff Ranch in Washoe Valley came from Folson & Bragg Sawmill in Reno. Folson & Bragg Sawmill was located in west Reno and, by 1887, was referred to as the "old Bragg lumber yard." The blacksmith shop was demolished sometime after the 1950s. (Nevada Historical Society, wa00525.)

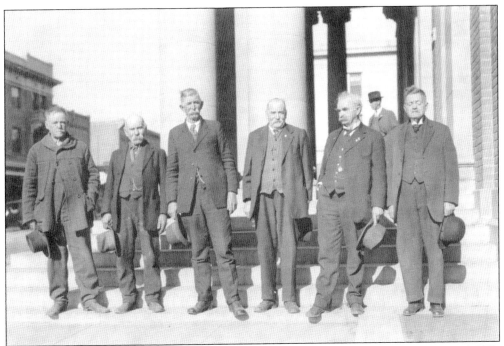

WASHOE COUNTY PIONEERS. George Peckham, S. Sellers, Jess Drake, Orville Sessions, Col. H.B. Maxon, and M.H. Virdin, all Washoe County pioneers, are shown standing on the courthouse steps in 1920. (Nevada Historical Society, wa03420.)

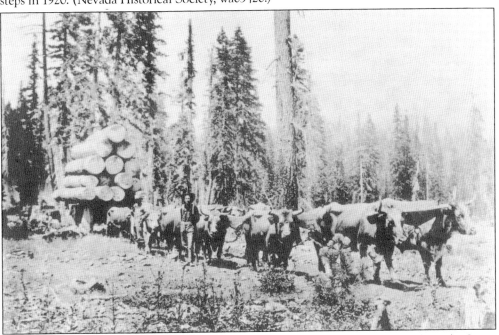

LOGGING WITH OX TEAMS. Teams of 20 to 30 oxen were used to transport logs from the Sierra Nevada to the sawmills. Lumber was used to build the "square-set" Deidesheimer timbering to support the underground structures of the mines and to supply steam power for the mills. (Nevada Historical Society, lum00538.)

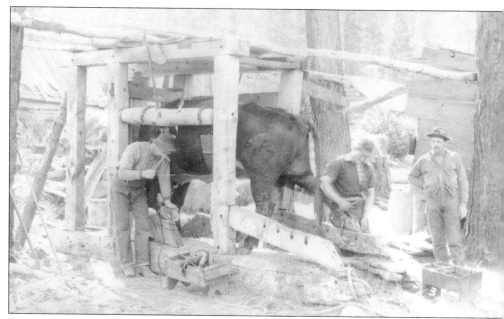

Shoeing an Ox. Oxen—slow, dependable animals—were used to pull extremely heavy loads of timber to the saw mills. Oxen required little care, but they did need to be shod to pull heavy loads. An ox was driven into the enclosure of the chute and the hoof was tied onto the block to allow men to examine the feet, trim the hoofs, and shoe the ox. (Nevada Historical Society, wa06621.)

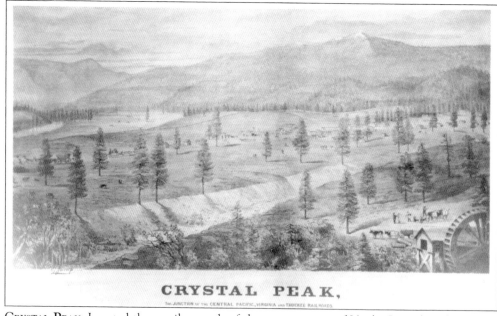

Crystal Peak. Located three miles north of the present town of Verdi, Crystal Peak was laid out in 1864 to be near the gold, coal, and timber found in nearby Dog Valley, California. The Central Pacific Railroad bypassed the town in 1868 to move across the Truckee River to the present site of Verdi. A sawmill is in the foreground, with a brewery in the center. (Nevada Historical Society, wa00889.)

VERDI MILL COMPANY AD. This advertisement in the *Wadsworth Dispatch* says that the company supplies flooring, ceiling, rustic, bevel siding, and surface lumber. The Verdi Lumber Company began as a railroad tie producer for the Southern Pacific Railroad in the 1880s. Oliver Lonkey, owner of a sawmill in Truckee, moved his company to Verdi in 1888. (Nevada State Library and Archives.)

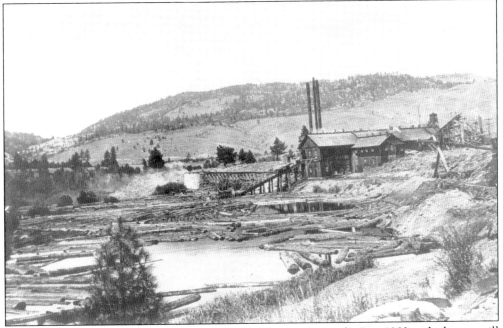

VERDI LUMBER COMPANY. Verdi was called a "lumberman's paradise" in 1902 with the sawmill employing 45 men and 50 more working in the woods. In 1910, the Verdi Lumber Company employed 350 men in a town with a population of 500. An article in the *Reno Gazette Journal* in January 1913 said that a "specialty of the company is the furnishing complete of all the materials needed in the construction of a building." (Nevada Historical Society, lum00065.)

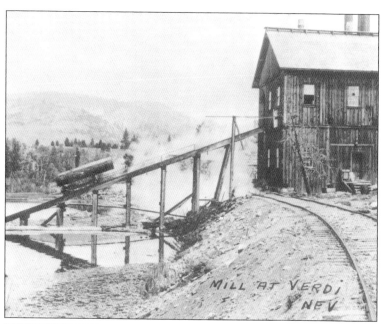

VERDI MILL, 1915. This photograph shows a log being lifted from the millpond to the saw mill. Flumes and a 40-mile standard gauge railroad brought timber from Dog Valley, California, to the mill. Ice gathered from ponds was another industry for Verdi. A fire in 1926 destroyed the town, and the Verdi Lumber Company closed in 1927. (Nevada Historical Society, wa09573.)

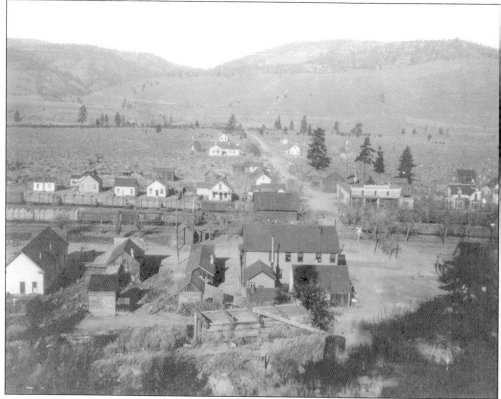

VERDI, 1898. A view of Verdi in 1898 is shown with the Central Pacific train going through the town. As a lumber town, Verdi had multiple fires that resulted in loss of the box factory in 1902, loss of a whole city block in 1903, loss of 42 homes in 1916, and in 1926, the loss of the lumber mill, roundhouse, storage yard, and school. (Nevada Historical Society, wa06975.)

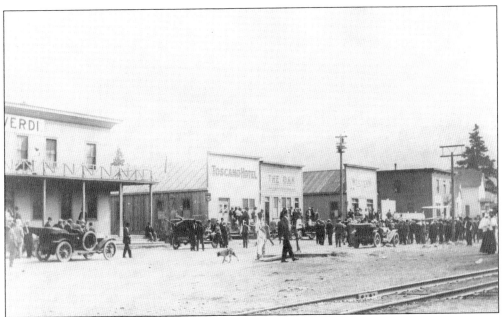

VERDI MAIN STREET. Verdi was named for the composer Giuseppe Verdi by the Central Pacific Railroad officials who opened a station there in 1868. The first post office was opened on November 30, 1869. This photograph shows the main street in Verdi in 1908. Verdi Glen, a summer resort in Verdi in 1932, had a dance pavilion, swimming pool, dining room, and cottages. (Nevada Historical Society, wa00659.)

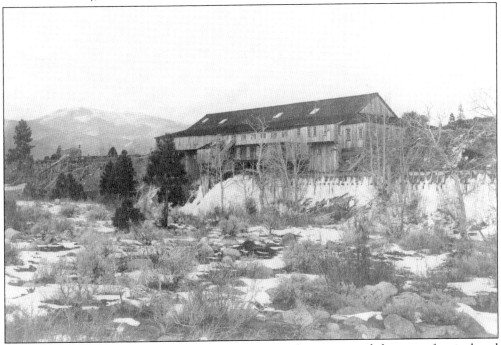

VERDI BOX FACTORY. The box factory produced boxes for storage and shipping of agricultural products. In 1904, the box factory and planing mill were sold to the California Pine Box and Lumber Company, a subsidiary of the Verdi Lumber Company. (Nevada Historical Society, lum00075.)

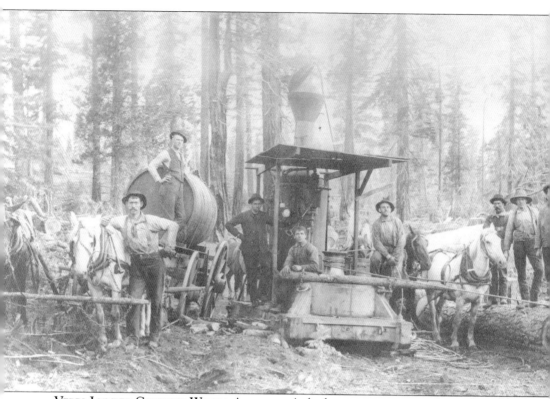

VERDI LUMBER COMPANY WOODS ACTIVITY. A donkey steam engine with winch and boiler is being used by the Verdi Lumber Company in the early 1900s near Dog Valley, California. The Verdi Lumber Company had men working in the box factory, sawmill, and lumber camps who made a salary of $5 to $15 per day in 1873. Sawmills located along the Truckee River cut 44 million board feet of lumber in 1888. A fire in 1888 at the Verdi Lumber Company reduced their cutting to 3.5 million board feet. Other sawmills along the Truckee River were the Lewison & Smith, George Schaffer, Elle Ellen, Richardson Brothers, Boca Mill Company, Truckee Lumber Company in Verdi and Truckee, Pacific Lumber and Wood Company, Hamlin and Doane, Boca Mill Company, and Richardson Brothers. (Nevada Historical Society, lum00071.)

Four

RAILROADS, HIGHWAYS, AND AIRPLANES

Early emigrants came to Washoe County on the Applegate-Lassen trail and the California trail from the 1840s until the 1860s. Pioneers stayed to establish trading posts and ranches. The California gold rush in 1849 and the Comstock gold and silver rushes in 1859 and 1873 brought miners and prospectors to the county. In 1868, the completion of the Central Pacific portion of the transcontinental railroad brought railway workers to Verdi, Mogul, Reno, and Wadsworth and more settlers to the county. The Virginia & Truckee Railroad connecting the mines of Virginia City to Carson City in 1868 and Reno to Carson City in 1872 brought an end to the Washoe Valley towns of Ophir, Franktown, and Washoe City. Sparks was founded in 1904 when the Central Pacific Railroad became the Southern Pacific Railroad, moving its headquarters from Wadsworth to a ranch east of Reno.

The Ophir and Geiger Grade toll roads provided access for the ranchers and merchants in Reno to the mines in Virginia City. The earliest road destined for the tourist trade was the Lake Tahoe Road. An article in the *Nevada State Journal* in March 1892 said, "It will make Reno the chief point of tourist travel, all of whom will leave more or less money here." By 1913, an article in the *Reno Evening Gazette* said, "Automobiling in Nevada is becoming a most popular pastime for owners of automobiles and a matter of profit to the various towns and cities of the state." Completion of the Victory Highway (US 40) and Lincoln Highway (US 50) in 1927 and the Three Flags Highway (US 395) in the early 1930s allowed for increased automobile and truck traffic into and out of the county.

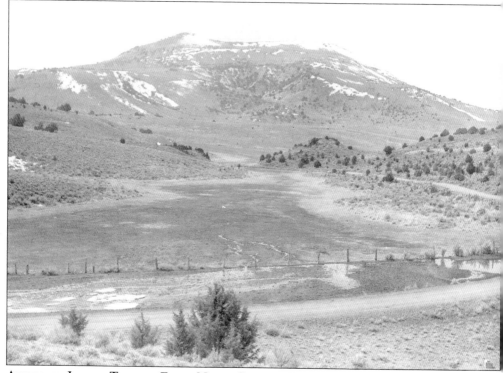

APPLEGATE-LASSEN TRAIL IN FORTY-NINER CANYON. Forty-Niner Canyon southeast of Vya in northern Washoe Canyon was named by the immigrants going to California in 1849. Alonzo Delano in his journal in 1849 said that mountains covered with cedars and firs could be seen from the trail. (Nevada Historical Society, trails00005.)

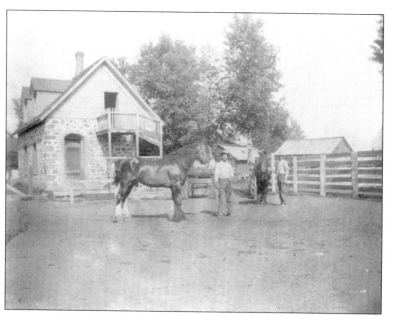

LESTER AND CHARLES JONES. Lester and Charles Jones are shown on the Jones Ranch in Glendale with two of their horses. (Nevada Historical Society, wa05512.)

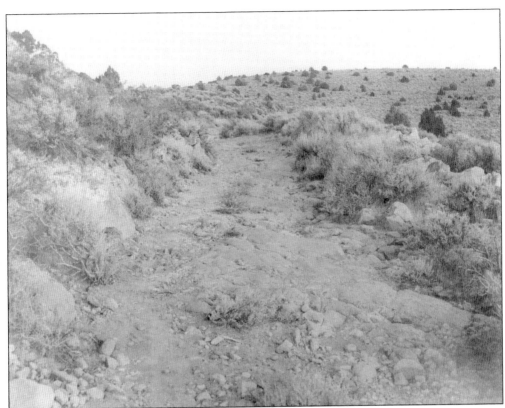

OPHIR TOLL ROAD. A historic road connecting the mines of Virginia City with the sawmills and quartz mills of Washoe Valley, the Ophir toll road or Ophir Causeway ran between Little Washoe Lake and Big Washoe Lake with the toll bridge mounted on pilings. Andy Russell was an early toll collector. The establishment of the Virginia & Truckee Railroad ended the use of the toll road except for hunters and fishermen coming into the valley. (Nevada Historical Society, toll roads 9.)

OLD GEIGER GRADE. The 1861 Nevada Territorial Legislature approved an act to collect tolls on roads and regulate franchises and rates. In the 1860s, toll road fees were $2 per wagon with one span of two horses, 25¢ for each extra horse, and $1.50 per person on horseback. Oxen and horse-drawn teams pulled wagons filled with supplies to Virginia City on this road. (Nevada Historical Society, wa00865.)

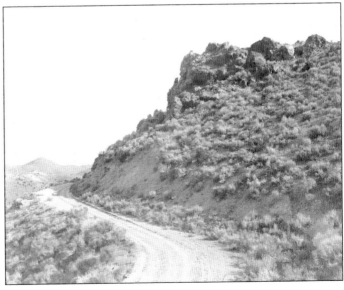

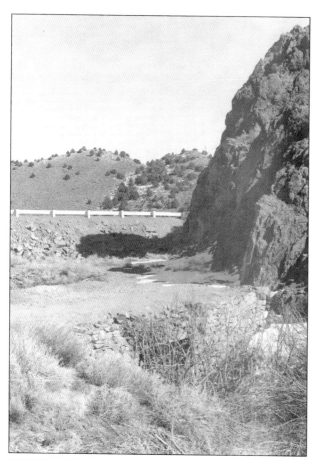

GEIGER TOLL ROAD, 1940. The Geiger Toll Road was constructed by Davison Geiger and John Tilton in 1862. In 1936, a new Geiger grade was completed that was to eliminate the dangerous curves of the old road. The new road was part of the scenic loop between Reno, Virginia City, Silver City, Carson City, and Washoe Valley. Geiger grade climbed 1,800 feet from the valley floor of the Truckee Meadows to Virginia City. In 1936, the new road cost $116,700.80. (Nevada Historical Society, wa00888.)

SOUTHERN PACIFIC RAILROAD STATION, RENO. The Central Pacific Railroad was seeking a Truckee Meadows site for a station to service Virginia City. Myron Lake wanted the station at Lake's Crossing, so he deeded 40 acres to Central Pacific Railroad. This site became the city of Reno. The first train through Reno was on June 18, 1868. (Southerland Collection.)

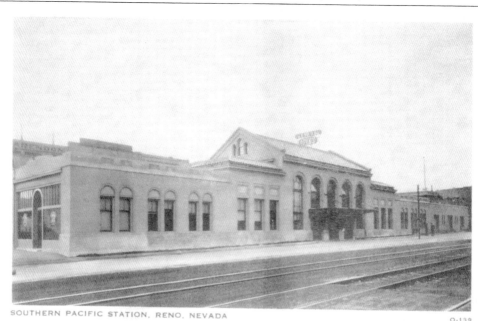

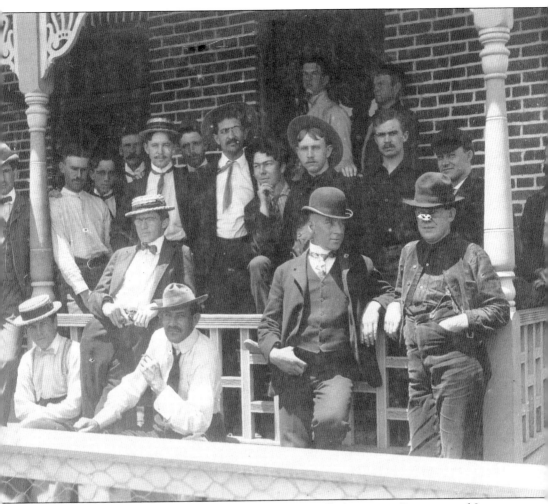

SOUTHERN PACIFIC OFFICE WORKERS. Wadsworth, originally known as Drytown and Lower Emigrant Crossing, was named after James S. Wadsworth, a Civil War general. There were very few buildings in 1868, but by 1900, Wadsworth was the second largest town in Washoe County and was an important railroad town. Residents in Wadsworth were employed in freighting, fishing in Pyramid Lake, cattle and sheep ranching, railroading, and mining. Wadsworth's population in 1900 was 1,309. Wadsworth had hotels, saloons, restaurants, grocery stores, and merchandise and variety stores, along with churches, schools, a library, and fraternal organizations such as the Knights of Pythias. By 1905, after the railroad moved to Sparks, Wadsworth was deserted except for one or two saloons and a few houses. Shown here are the office workers in Wadsworth in 1902 before the move to Sparks. (Nevada Historical Society, wa00743.)

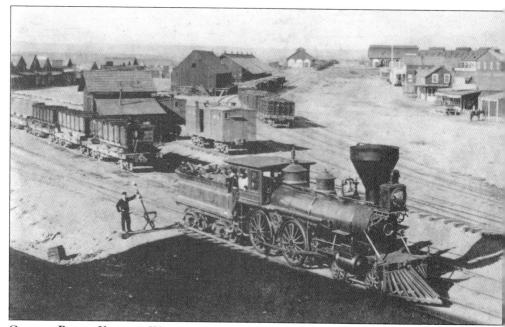

CENTRAL PACIFIC YARDS AT WADSWORTH. Central Pacific Railroad had a work camp in Wadsworth in 1868 to help build the transcontinental railroad to Promontory Point, Utah. Wadsworth became the rail stop for the Truckee Division in 1868. Trains stopped at Wadsworth to get wood and water before crossing the Forty Mile Desert. Wadsworth was one of the largest towns in Washoe County at that time. (Nevada Historical Society, rr-105.)

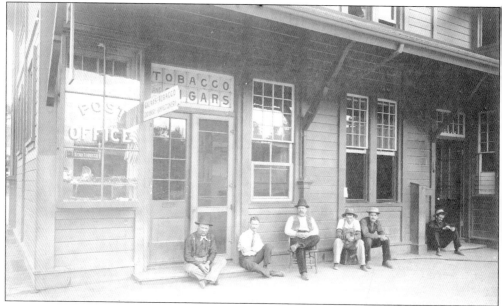

WADSWORTH DEPOT AND POST OFFICE, 1889. The railroad roundhouse and shops employed several men. The Wadsworth Post Office opened on August 20, 1868. The population in 1870 was 253, but Wadsworth had grown to 661 by 1880. The railroad relocated its shops to east of the Truckee in 1882. A fire in Wadsworth in April 1884 destroyed the original shops. (Nevada Historical Society, wa00709.)

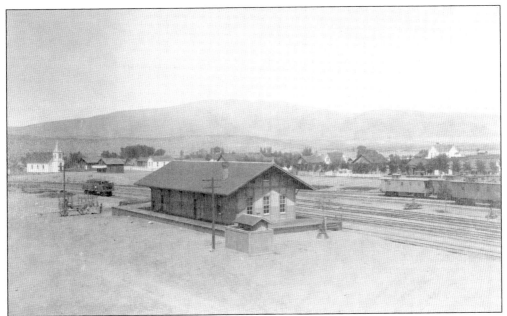

WADSWORTH, 1895. Miners and prospectors stopped at Wadsworth for supplies before going to mining camps in Churchill, Esmeralda, Mineral, and Nye Counties. Freight companies began hauling supplies to these camps and often hauled ore back to be shipped by train from Wadsworth. (Nevada Historic Society, wa00682.)

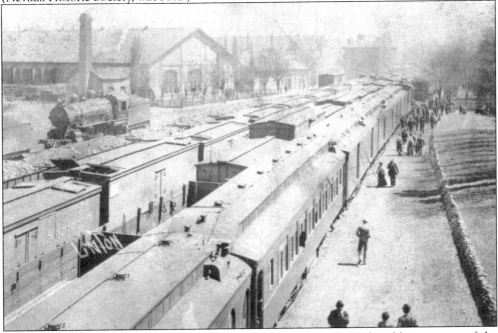

SOUTHERN PACIFIC RAILROAD, WADSWORTH. The Central Pacific Railroad became part of the Southern Pacific Railroad Company in the early 1900s. The shops built in Wadsworth in 1882 were outdated by the 1900s, so Southern Pacific, trying to save money, decided to close the Wadsworth shops to move to a ranch east of Reno that later would become the city of Sparks. (Nevada Historical Society, rr00202.)

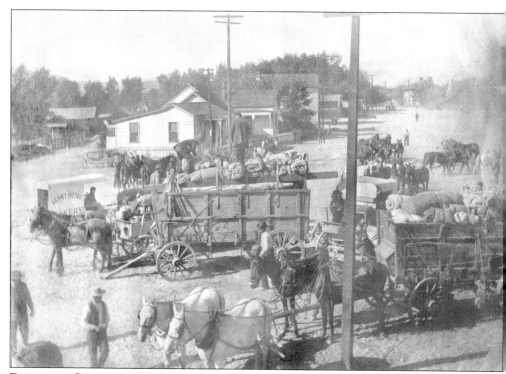

FREIGHTING CONTRACTORS MOVING WADSWORTH. The houses for the railroad workers were taken apart board by board, placed on flatcars along with furniture, cows, pets, and trees and garden plants, then taken to the new location east of Reno. More than 300 workers left Wadsworth between 1902 and 1905. (Nevada Historical Society, wa00689.)

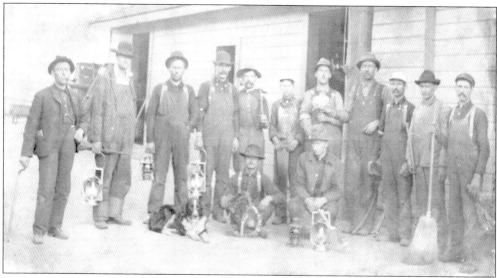

SOUTHERN PACIFIC RAILROAD WORKERS, SPARKS. A fire in Wadsworth in 1902 and the lack of a good water supply, along with trying to save money, prompted Southern Pacific Railroad to move to Sparks. Sparks was first named Harriman but was renamed in 1905 by the Nevada legislature to honor Gov. John Sparks. Shown here are some of the workers who moved to Sparks. (Nevada Historical Society, RR 01668.)

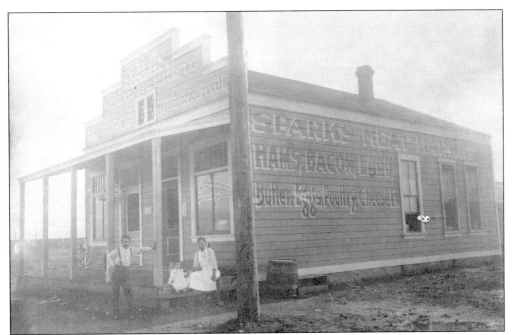

SPARKS MEAT MARKET. Businesses in the Truckee Meadows prepared for the move of the railroad workers from Wadsworth to the new town of Sparks. Shown here is a meat market in 1902 that was built by Sardis M. Summerfield. From left to right are Summerfield, daughter Esther, and an unidentified clerk. (Nevada Historical Society, wa04403.)

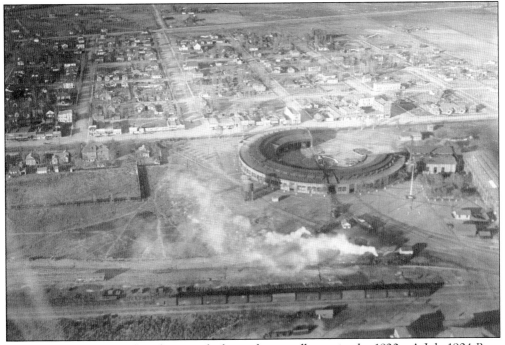

SPARKS ROUNDHOUSE. This photograph shows the roundhouse in the 1920s. A July 1904 *Reno Evening Gazette* article described the world's largest turntable in Sparks, saying its "perfect symmetry resembled the Roman Colosseum [sic]." (Nevada Historical Society, wa00569.)

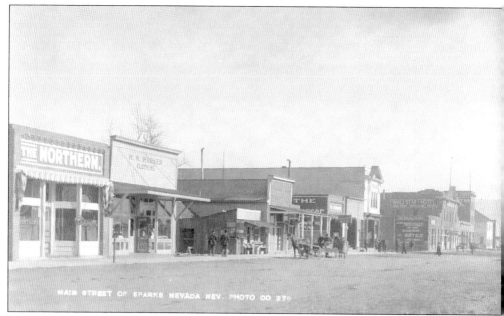

MAIN STREET, SPARKS. Sparks, in the early 1900s, is shown looking at a block on B Street where the Wallstab Hotel was located. Charles Wallstab opened the hotel after moving from Wadsworth in the early 1900s. The hotel had a fountain in the lobby with a goldfish pond. A lunch room, dining room, and bakery were in the hotel. Charles Wallstab leased all of this B Street block except for the building housing the Crystal Saloon. (Southerland Collection.)

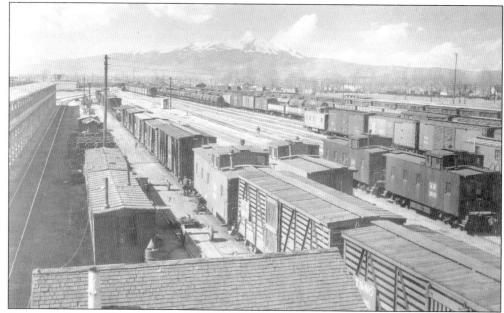

SOUTHERN PACIFIC RAILROAD, SPARKS. The Southern Pacific Railroad was the largest employer in Sparks in 1944, with a monthly payroll of $400,000. The Sparks division linked Salt Lake City with Sacramento. Large, cab-ahead locomotives crossing the Sierra Nevada were serviced and changed to lighter engines that went east. Employees inspected and serviced the passenger and freight trains and re-iced refrigerator cars. (Nevada State Library and Archives, PLA-0071.)

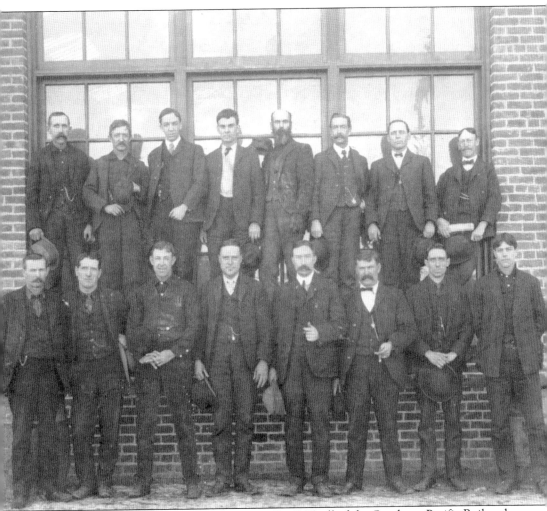

SOUTHERN PACIFIC RAILROAD WORKERS, SPARKS. By 1905, all of the Southern Pacific Railroad workers and their families from Wadsworth had moved to Sparks. Shown are, from left to right, (first row) R.H. Davis, boiler foreman; J.C. Carrigan, erecting foreman; W.R. Ashby, roundhouse foreman; F.C. Kerin, assistant master mechanic; G.F. Goble, general foreman; W.J. McEnerny, car foreman; C.V. Cheney, blacksmith foreman; and M.J. Hier, assistant boiler foreman; (second row) J. Larson, carpenter foreman; J.H. Sullivan, pipe foreman; C. Thornburn, storekeeper; C.W. Dresser, assistant roundhouse foreman; J.M. Blanchard, painter foreman; H.L. Luttrell, general foreman's clerk; J.A. Breen, machine foreman; and W.C. Wilson, gallery foreman. (Nevada Historical Society, RR 164.)

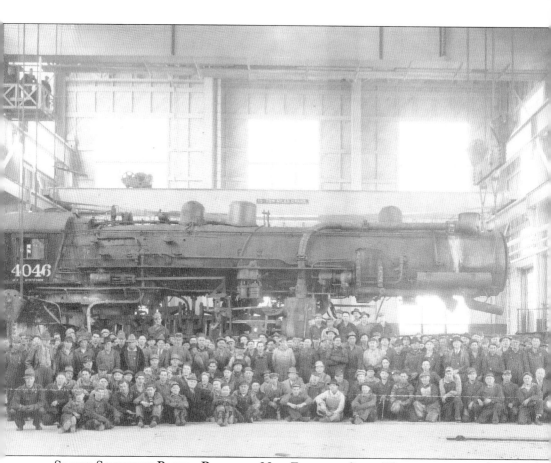

SPARKS SOUTHERN PACIFIC RAILROAD NEW ERECTING SHOP. The new erecting shop for the Southern Pacific Railroad in Sparks was opened in 1944. The shop was used to overhaul the largest locomotives in the Southern Pacific fleet. It had a 200-ton-capacity traveling crane in a building that was 250 feet long, 90 feet wide, and 70 feet high. The crane, thought to be the largest in the world, lifted the locomotives up and placed them in one of 11 repair pits that were 58 feet long. The Southern Pacific Railroad in Sparks employed 1,447 workers but hoped to add 274 additional employees with the new erecting shop. The remodeling of the Sparks shops added larger machine shops, a 40-stall roundhouse, and car shops. In 1942, Southern Pacific Railroad had 973 miles of track in Nevada and paid $1.2 million in state taxes. (Nevada State Library and Archives, PLA-069.)

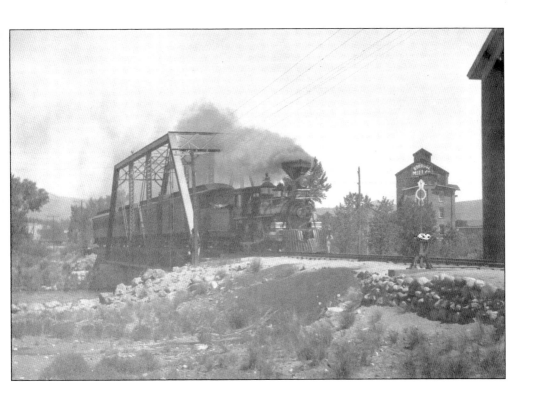

VIRGINIA & TRUCKEE RAILROAD. Above is a photograph of Engine 22. Work was started on the Virginia & Truckee Railroad to extend it from Carson City to Reno in June 1871. Stops were at Lakeview, Mill Station, Franktown, Washoe City, Steamboat Springs, Browns, and Huffakers. The Virginia & Truckee Railroad entered Reno on the east side of Virginia Street to meet up with the Central Pacific Railroad at the Depot Hotel. Below is a Virginia & Truckee Railroad ticket from Carson City to Mill Station on the north end of Washoe Valley, dated 1878. A special price for a roundtrip ticket on July 4, 1908, was $1.50. The regular price for a roundtrip ticket was $3. (Above, Nevada Historical Society, RR-01535; below, Dan Webster collection.)

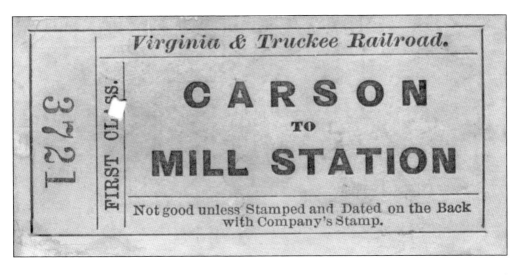

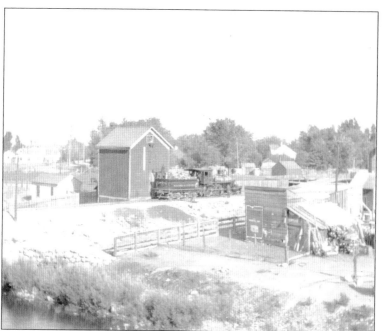

VIRGINIA & TRUCKEE RAILROAD. This Virginia & Truckee Railroad train was stopped to get water at a tank in Reno in 1907. The 18.01-mile track from Reno to Carson City was finished in August 1872. Freight and passenger services were offered. (Nevada Historical Society, rr00525.)

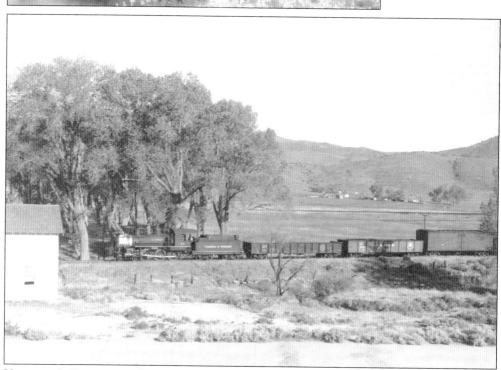

VIRGINIA & TRUCKEE AT STEAMBOAT SPRINGS. The natural hot springs at Steamboat Springs were discovered by Felix Monet in 1860. Dr. Edna J. Carver bought the springs in 1918 to make a health resort for those suffering from "rheumatic ailments and other ailments" and for athletic training. The boxers Paolino Uzcudin and King Levinski trained at the springs for their fights with Max Baer. Steamboat Springs was a railway stop for the Virginia & Truckee Railroad. (Nevada Historical Society, rr00539.)

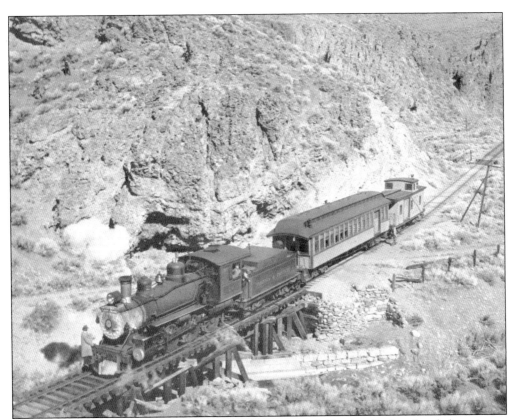

VIRGINIA & TRUCKEE IN WASHOE CANYON. The Virginia & Truckee Railroad ended service on May 11, 1950. This photograph was taken at the end of its run in the 1940s. (Nevada Historical Society, rr01528.)

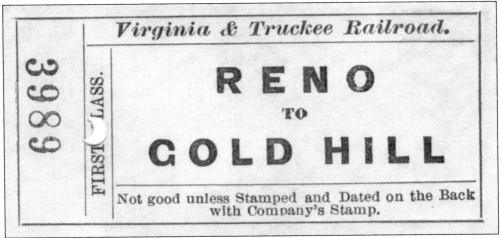

TICKET FROM RENO TO GOLD HILL. Above is a Virginia & Truckee Railroad ticket from Reno to Gold Hill. A passenger used this ticket to travel from Reno to Gold Hill on April 2, 1878. The back of the ticket is stamped with the Virginia & Truckee Railroad ticket office and the date. (Dan Webster collection.)

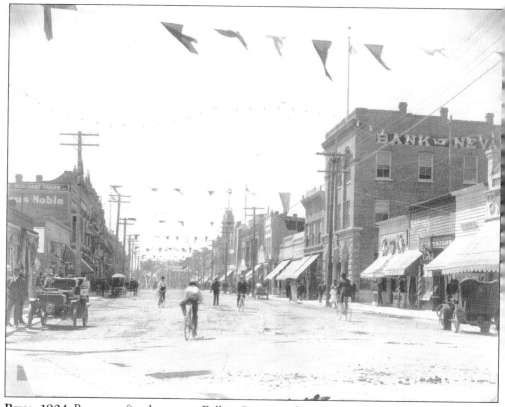

Reno, 1904. Reno was first known as Fullers Crossing after Charles W. Fuller, who built a hotel and a toll bridge over the Truckee River there in 1859. Myron C. Lake bought the toll bridge from Fuller, and later Reno became known as Lakes Crossing. Lake deeded land to Charles Crocker for the Central Pacific railway station and Reno was born. (Nevada Historical Society, wa02052.)

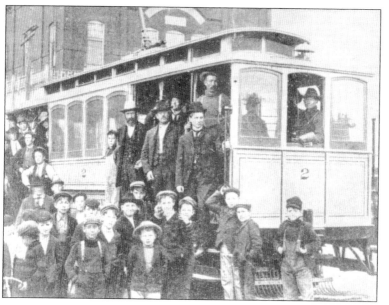

Electric Railroad. The Nevada Transit Company had a franchise to run the first electric railroad from Reno to Sparks in 1904. A *Reno Evening Gazette* editorial in July 1904 reported "it will be run for the benefit of the public." Sen. H.J. Darling paid for the first ticket and 3,000 rode on the first day on November 24, 1904. (Dan Webster collection.)

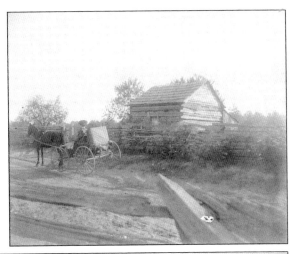

ON THE WAY TO CARSON CITY. Going from Reno to Carson City in 1906 was a treacherous undertaking. One of the first highway construction projects started by the Nevada Department of Highways in 1918 was the 9.52 miles from Huffakers to Washoe Summit. (Nevada Historical Society, wa04484)

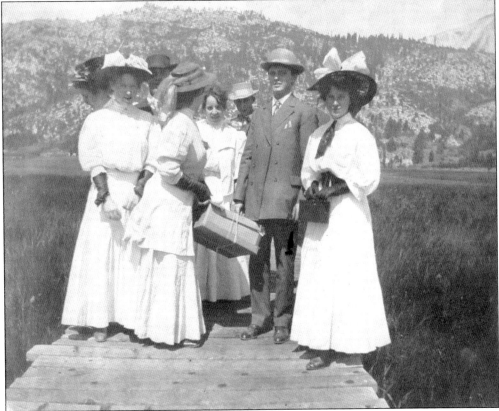

BOARDWALK NEAR BOWERS, 1908. Perhaps out for a day at Bowers Mansion, this group is returning to Reno or Carson City on the Virginia & Truckee Railroad. In 1903, Henry Riter, wanting to make a picnic resort, built a swimming pool and power plant at Bowers Mansion. School, church, business, and fraternal organization picnics were held on the well-maintained grounds. Bowers Mansion had a restaurant with a dance floor and bar. During Prohibition, the bar sold soft drinks along with bottled water from the Mansion's hot springs. Bowers Mansion was sold to the Reno Women's Civic League in 1946 and soon after became a Washoe County Park. (Nevada Historical Society, wa00070C.)

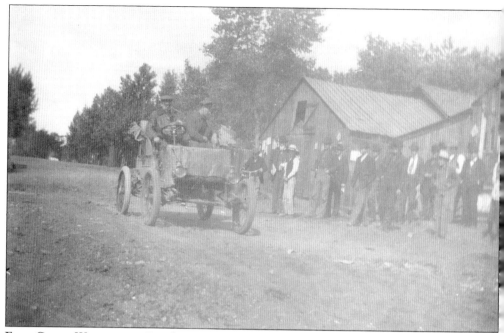

First Car in Wadsworth. People came out to see what was thought to be the first automobile in Wadsworth in 1903. The *Reno Evening Gazette* in May 1911 said, "there is an excellent automobile road between this city and Pyramid Lake." The road needed some repair but was "the best long auto road in this county." (Nevada Historical Society, trans-abs00045.)

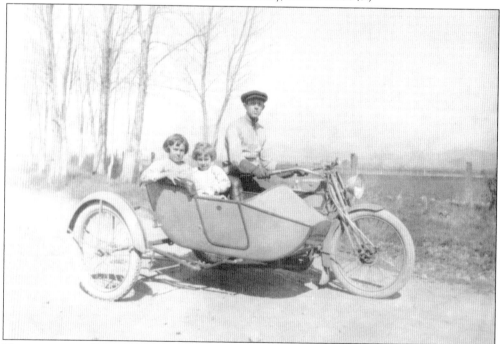

Motorcycle at Glendale. *The List of Registered Automobiles and Motorcycles* compiled by the Nevada secretary of state in 1916 shows this motorcycle registered to J.F. Kleppe of Reno with the license number 3034. (Nevada Historical Society, wa06534.)

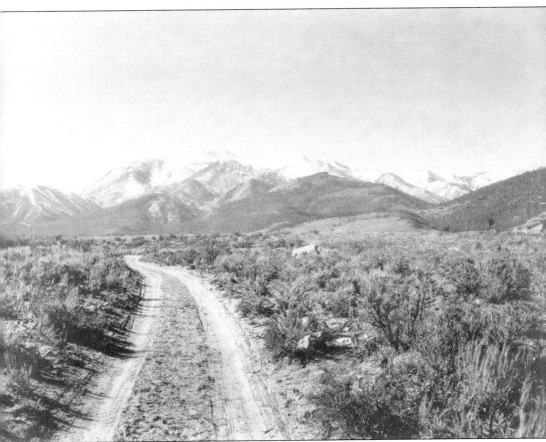

Mount Rose. There is a dispute over the naming of Mount Rose. Some claim it was named for Rose Hickman, friend of H.S. Ham, a printer for the *Washoe Times* newspaper, while others claim it was named for Jacob H. Rose, an early Franktown mill owner. Mount Rose is 10,778 feet above sea level. The *Washoe Weekly Times* of August 5, 1865, tells of some of the first to climb Mount Rose, reporting that Dr. G.A. Weed; Charles N. Harris, Esq.; Judge John W. North; Justice James F. Lewis; and "more women" said about the ascent: "It is quite a hard trip to make, particularly for ladies, but well repays the time and trouble it takes to view nature from her loftiest promontory." The party rode horses to within "one thousand feet of the summit," then walked the rest of the way. The paper reports that others were planning to climb Mount Rose. (Nevada Historical Society, wa00146.)

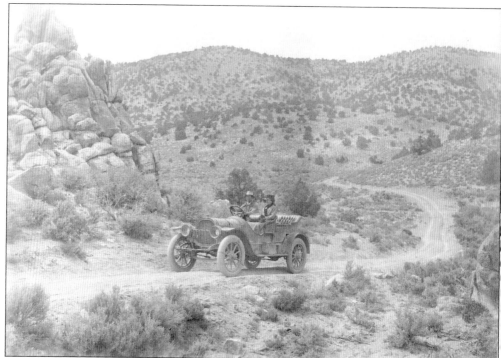

CAR ON TRAIL. Out for a drive in the country, this couple may have been on a trail in Washoe County in 1910. The purchase of an automobile at that time was considered an event worthy of publishing in the newspaper. Since there was no Nevada Department of Highways until 1918, the Nevada Good Roads Club was organized to help improve roads in Nevada. A statewide holiday was held in May 1914 so that residents could work together to improve Nevada roads. (Nevada Historical Society, trans-abs00067.)

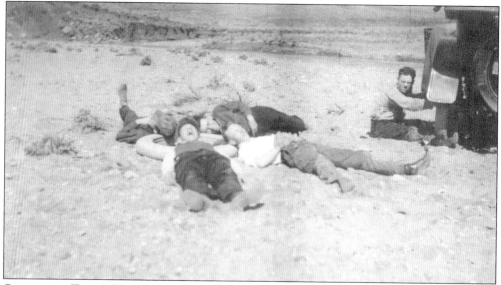

CHANGING A TIRE. Bill Holeswourth was changing a tire in 1919 in this photograph while friends are resting along the side of the road. Perhaps Bill should have taken advantage of the services provided by the Gerlach Hotel and Garage. (Nevada Historical Society, wa06492.)

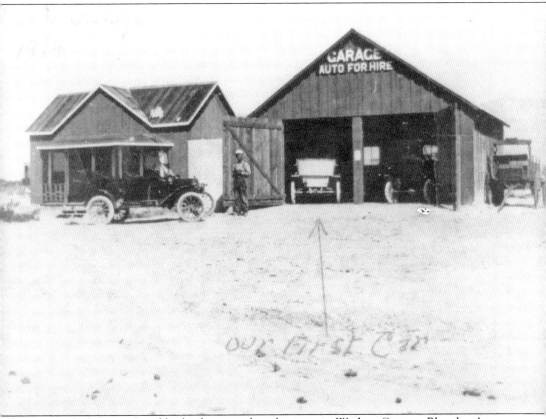

BLANCHETT'S GARAGE. Possibly the first rental car business in Washoe County, Blanchett's was offering a car for hire in 1914 in Gerlach. Guy Blanchett bought a new Ford from Calavada Auto Company, an authorized Ford dealer, in Reno in 1915. C.H. Lamb was the president and manager and J. M. Spalding was the secretary-treasurer of Calavada in 1915. The county commissioners voted to approve $10,000 to build a wagon road from Surprise Valley, California, to Gerlach. The commissioners hoped that Gerlach "would become an important trading place" between California and Leadville. The Gerlach Hotel and Garage was advertised as the "Headquarters for Traveling Man" with automotive services provided to any point in 1924. (Nevada Historical Society, wa00908.)

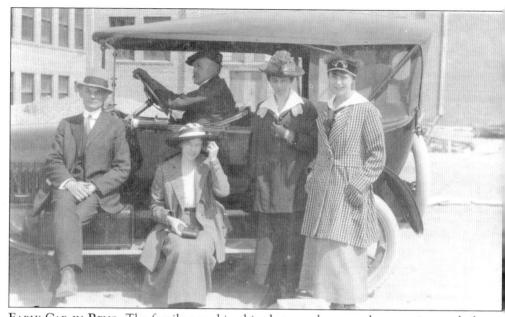

EARLY CAR IN RENO. The family posed in this photograph was perhaps getting ready for an "automobiling" outing on the Victory Highway or Lincoln Highway. If going on the Lincoln Highway, the family may have seen a sign that was a 22-inch circle with the top three inches painted red and the bottom three inches painted blue with black lettering. Capt. Harry Gosse, the proprietor of the Riverside Hotel, provided the stencils for the signs. (Nevada Historical Society, wa06488.)

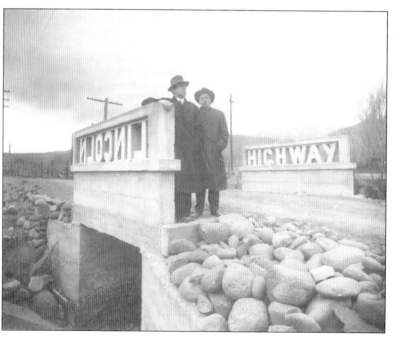

LINCOLN HIGHWAY BRIDGE IN VERDI. The Lincoln Highway followed the Truckee River from Wadsworth to Verdi. Here, H.E. Frederickson, an official for the Lincoln Highway, and J.O. Sessions, a Washoe County commissioner, dedicated the Verdi Lincoln Highway Bridge in 1914. (Nevada Historical Society, trans-hwy00372.)

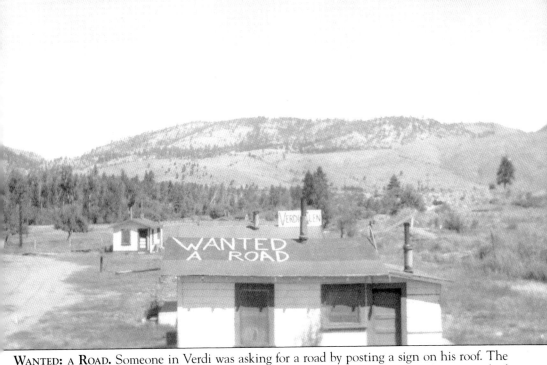

WANTED: A ROAD. Someone in Verdi was asking for a road by posting a sign on his roof. The Nevada Good Roads Club in 1914 and 1916, in an effort to improve the roads in the county, had volunteer workers in Verdi help repair the Dog Valley grade. Workers were told to "come with a pick, rake, and shovel." The 1919 Nevada legislature allowed the Washoe County Commission to issue bonds to resurface the road from the California border through Verdi, Reno, Sparks, and Wadsworth. The California State Highway Commission, with much controversy, chose to build a road from Verdi to Truckee through Dog Valley in 1921. In 1940, US Highway 40 was completed between Truckee, California, and Reno following the Truckee River, and the route through Dog Valley was abandoned. Interstate 80 later followed this same route. (Nevada Historical Society, wa00677.)

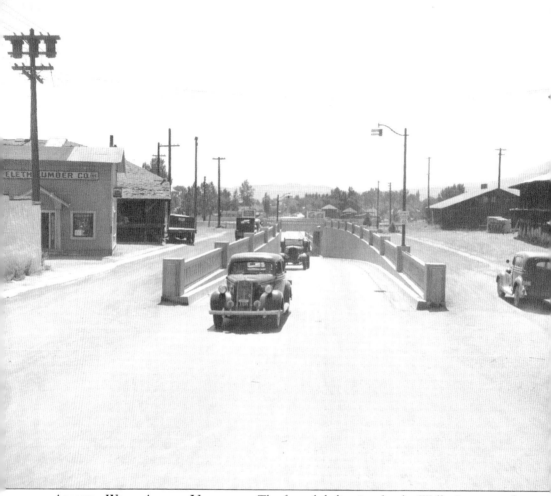

ALAMEDA-WELLS AVENUE UNDERPASS. The formal dedication for the Wells Avenue underpass was on September 10, 1937. The underpass was built for $200,000, with all but $750 coming from the federal government. Built to replace the old cattle bridge on Park Street, the underpass was to be safer and offer an optional route for those using East Fourth Street or the Victory Highway (US 40). According to an article in the 1937 *Nevada Highways and Parks*, the underpass was 200 feet long, with the bridge unit at 188 feet long. The underpass was the "largest of its kind" in Nevada. There were 26,446 cubic yards of "roadway excavation work, 2,335 cubic yards of structural excavation, 5,031 square yards of sub-grading, 1,320 cubic yards of crushed gravel or stone surfacing, and 242 cubic yards of crushed gravel or stone surfacing material for the footpaths." Over 100 laborers for the underpass project came from the rolls of the Reno reemployment office. (Nevada Historical Society, wa02310.)

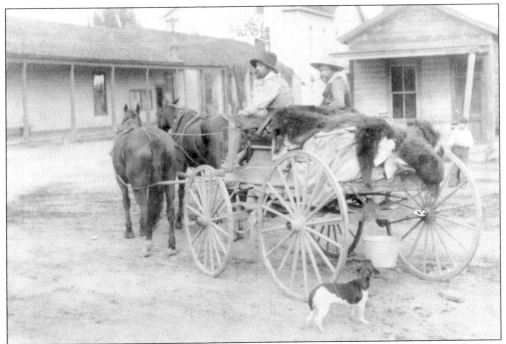

WAGON WITH BEAR HIDE. In 1900, these men are shown on a wagon in Reno with a bear hide in the back. Black bears lived in the Sierra Nevada, as they do today. These bears weigh approximately 500 pounds and are cinnamon or black in color. The Nevada Bear Club often hunted in Grizzly Valley in Plumas County, California. (Nevada Historical Society, wa01006.)

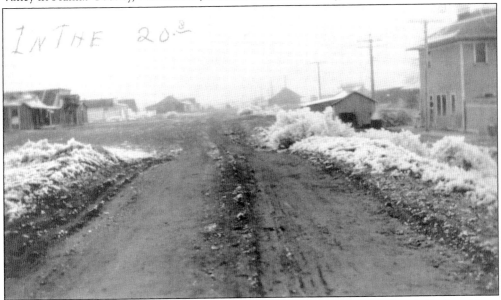

MAIN STREET, GERLACH. Gerlach was a division terminal for the Western Pacific Railroad from 1910 to 1932. Main Street, running parallel to the railroad tracks, was owned by the Western Pacific Railroad, which leased the homes and businesses to the residents for what was considered a moderate price. Bruno's Country Club, owned by Bruno Selmi, opened in July 1952. (Nevada Historical Society, wa06258.)

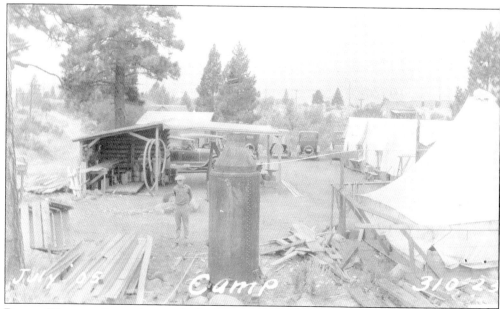

BRIDGE WORKERS CAMP. A camp for highway workers building a bridge over the Truckee River near Verdi on July 5, 1925, is shown. The Verdi Bridge, located one-half mile west of US Highway 40, was finished in 1928 for $15,447.50. In a 1984 interview, Thomas W. Macaulay of Macaulay Iron Works, which constructed the bridge, said it contained 3,600 rivets. (Nevada Historical Society, trans-hwy00858.)

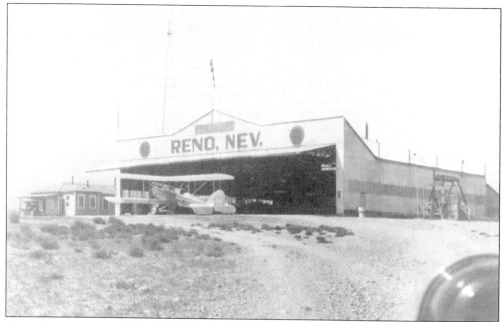

FIRST RENO AIRPORT. Blanchfield Field, the first Reno airport, was located near the present Washoe County Golf Course on Urban and Arlington Streets. Hubbard Field, the second airport, was capable of handling larger passenger planes and, in 1936, included parts of the Kietzke, Carameila, Damonte, Steele, and Matley Ranches. Hubbard Field is now part of the Reno Tahoe International Airport. (Nevada Historical Society, wa01217.)

Five

SCHOOLS, CHURCHES, AND PICNICS

Schools and churches in Washoe County followed the mining camps, railroad camps, and ranches. Nevada had a transient population of miners, prospectors, and mill workers who found it difficult to attend regular church services. Some miners, prospectors, and railway workers were single, but many brought their wives and children with them. The early families wanted churches and schools in Washoe County like the places they had left behind. The *Appletree* of May 9, 1976 stated, "Early Nevada clergymen were an enterprising lot, quite willing to preach in a saloon if no other facilities were available or to walk a 200-mile circuit, deliver a baby, face down a gunman or deal with any other emergency. They were truly men for any occasion." T.H. McGrath built the Methodist Episcopal church, which was the first protestant church in Washoe City, in 1863. The Catholic church held High Mass as early as 1867 in the courthouse in Washoe City. A small Catholic church was built in Washoe Valley in 1868. Reverend F.M. Willis would ride a horse with a broken saddle to Glendale to preach and Father Manogue was known to administer the last rites to a man about to be hanged. Mining camps and ranching communities often held services in saloons, tents, lodging houses, schools, or railway cars.

The Franktown School was the earliest school built in the Nevada Territory in 1857. The Washoe County schools of Glendale, Mill Station, Huffakers, and Browns soon followed. Parochial schools came next, like the Whitaker School, an Episcopal seminary for girls in Reno near Washington Street and Terrace Drive, which was built in 1874.

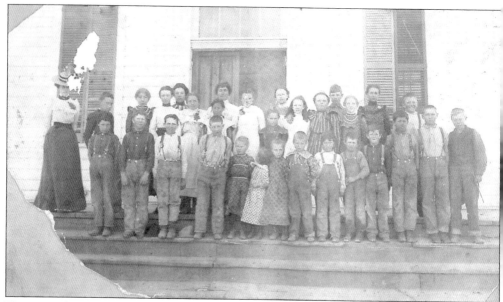

HUFFAKER SCHOOL. Granville Huffaker and Stephen Ede were farmers in the area who deeded land for the school building in the 1870s. The school, with a bell tower, had one room for the first through eighth grades and one teacher. Students attending the school in 1898 are in this photograph. (Nevada Historical Society, ed01265.)

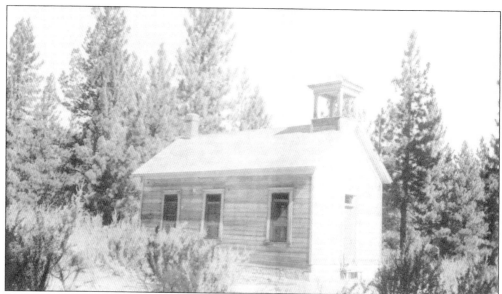

MILL STATION SCHOOL. The Mill Station School was built for the children of the mill workers living between Carson City and Washoe City in the 1860s. George Hoopengarner was the teacher in 1862. Ira Clark was the teacher at the new schoolhouse built in 1878. Ross Lewers was the clerk of the board of trustees. The school was consolidated with the Franktown School in 1889. (Nevada Historical Society, ed00352.)

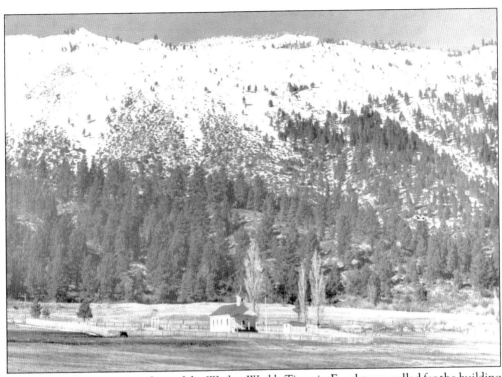

FRANKTOWN SCHOOL. An editor of the *Washoe Weekly Times* in Franktown called for the building of a school in 1863 saying, "We must have a schoolhouse—and the quicker we have it, the better." The Franktown School, built in 1857 of logs, was the first school in the Nevada Territory. This photograph shows a later school that was a white, one-room building surrounded by a picket fence. G.H. Douglas was clerk of the board of trustees and W.R. Anglemeyer was the teacher in 1878. Crissie Andrews (Caughlin) and Persia Bowers attended the school in the 1870s. The school had 11 students in 1956, its last year. The building was a community center from 1956 until it burned in August 1963. (Nevada Historical Society, ed00355.)

GALENA CREEK SCHOOL. Galena, located 14 miles south of Reno at the base of the Steamboat Hills, was a lumber producer for the Comstock mines. Elma Gould, one of the last teachers at the one-room Galena Creek School in 1956, said that she prepared different lessons for each student. In 1956, there were 14 students in eight grades. (Nevada Historical Society, ed00365.)

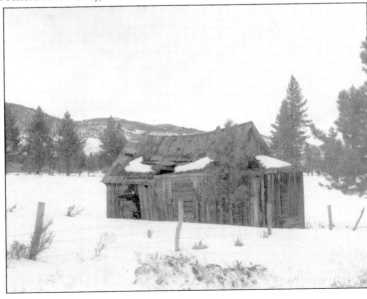

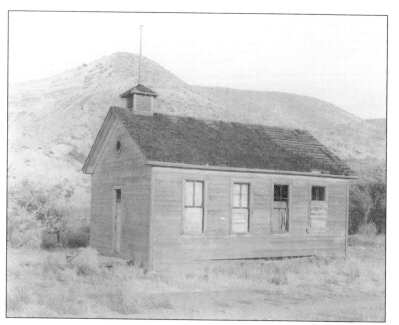

MOGUL SCHOOL. Located between Verdi and Lawton, Mogul was a station for the Southern Pacific Railroad. Children of railroad workers attended this one-room school. (Nevada Historical Society, ed00363.)

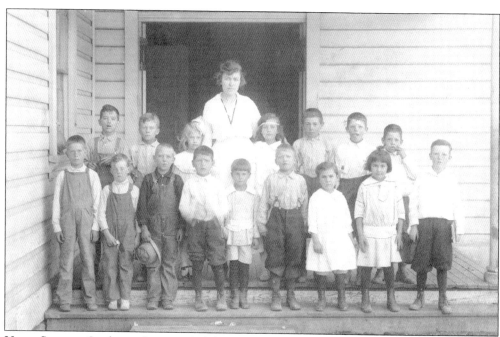

VERDI SCHOOL. Students who attended the Verdi School in 1916 are shown in this photograph with their teacher, Mila Coffin. This school burned in the Verdi fire of 1926, to be replaced by a new school designed by George A. Ferris, a Reno architect, in 1928. The Verdi earthquake of December 29, 1948, damaged the 1928 school. The Verdi School had eight grades in two rooms with about 40 students in 1956. (Nevada Historical Society, ed01259.)

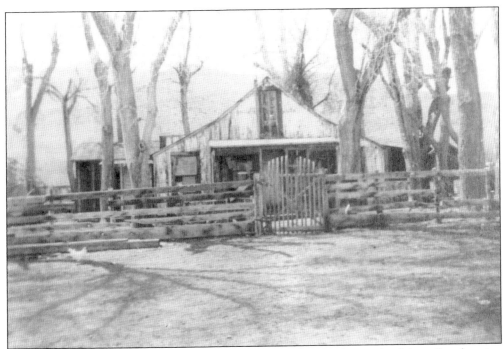

BONHAM RANCH SCHOOL. Located at the Bonham Ranch, 14 miles north of the railroad station in Flanigan, the Bonham Ranch School first held classes in 1887. Few students were attending in 1919 when the school was closed, and the building later became a storage shed. Children from the area then went to the Bonham School in Flanigan. It was Washoe County's last one-room school, and closed on June 20, 1969. (Nevada Historical Society, wa05913.)

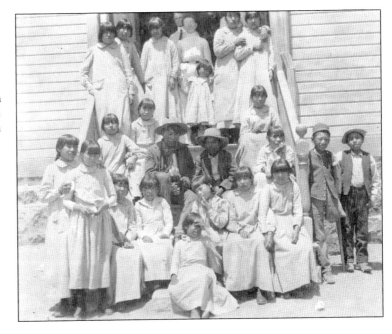

PYRAMID LAKE DAY SCHOOL. The Pyramid Lake Indian Day School or Natchez School was opened in Wadsworth in 1878 by the Bureau of Indian Affairs with one teacher. The school closed in 1893, reopened in 1899, and permanently closed in 1921. Reading, writing, and arithmetic were taught. The school was located in the Indian agency building. (Nevada Historical Society, eth00828.)

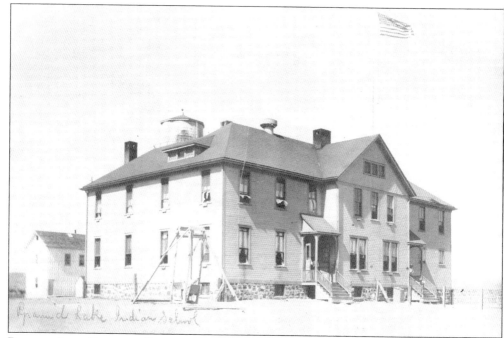

PYRAMID LAKE BOARDING SCHOOL. The Pyramid Lake Indian Boarding School opened in 1885 to teach vocational education to Indian students. The school included boys' and girls' dormitories, a dining hall, and a commissary. Students learned reading and writing in classrooms, then went to the laundry, sewing rooms, garden, mechanics shed, and kitchen for the vocational training. (Nevada Historical Society, eth00826.)

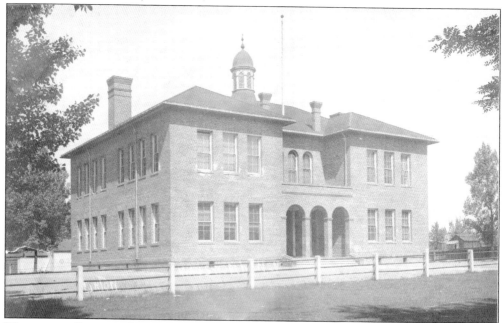

WADSWORTH SCHOOL. The cornerstone for the Wadsworth school was laid on July 26, 1899, with the school opening soon after. The school, with its three acres of land, was sold to the Pyramid Lake Indian Reservation in 1997. (Nevada Historical Society, ed00368.)

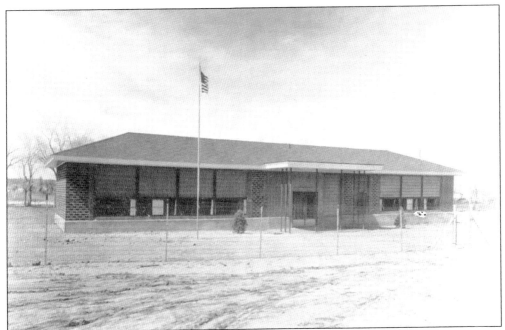

BROWN SCHOOL. Felix Brown deeded land for the Brown School, first built in 1878. Browns, an early stage station and later a Virginia & Truckee Railroad stop, was seven miles southeast of Reno. The first school was torn down in 1911. This photograph of a newer school was taken in 1948. (Nevada State Library and Archives, PLAN-0100.)

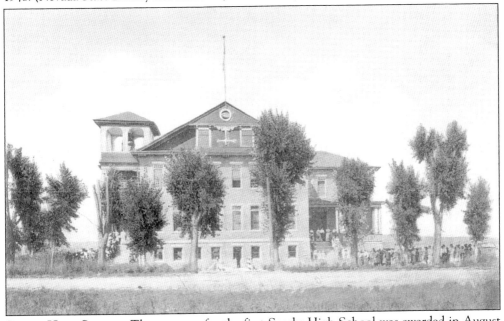

SPARKS HIGH SCHOOL. The contract for the first Sparks High School was awarded in August 1904. The High School, designed by architect H.E. Kronnick, was a two-story brick building with a basement. The first and second floors had four classrooms each. The office and library were on the first floor. The main entrance was below the tower on the southwest corner. (Southerland Collection.)

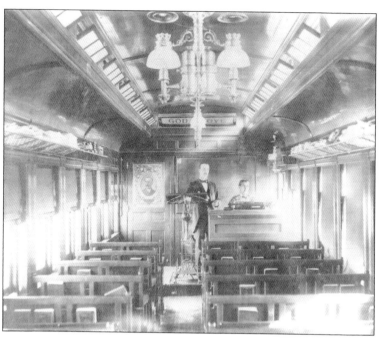

EMANUEL BAPTIST CHURCH. This "chapel car" church was a railway car used by the Baptist church that traveled from town to town on the railway. The "chapel cars" would pull off to a sidetrack for the services, then pull back to the railway to continue on to another community. The preacher and organist are preparing for a service in Wadsworth in 1896. (Nevada Historical Society, wa00719.)

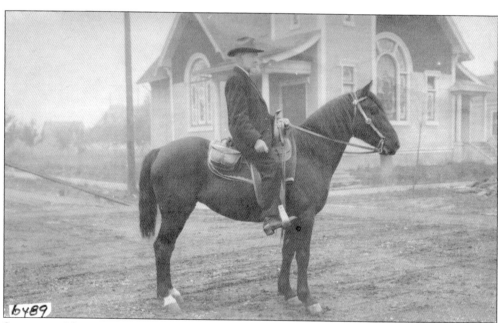

SADDLEBAG MISSIONARY. Outlying areas in Washoe County might have been served by saddlebag missionaries, or circuit riders, traveling on horses or mules from the Reno or Sparks churches to preach the gospel. Prospectors, miners, loggers, and farmers might listen to the sermon in a tent, hotel, school, or saloon. The Methodist church in Nevada was known for its saddlebag missionaries. (Nevada Historical Society, wa06489.)

Union Church at Wadsworth. Money was being raised in June 1888 to build the Union Church in Wadsworth. An article in the *Reno Evening Gazette* in 1892 reported that the church was "quite large and is much liked by everyone." (Nevada Historical Society, wa00722.)

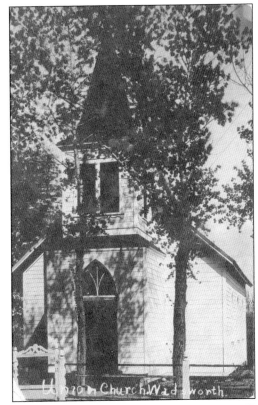

Easter in Wadsworth. The Union Church in Wadsworth is decorated for a special service in the late 1880s. The decoration may have been for Easter or for a fundraising at the church. In 1892, Wadsworth townspeople held benefits to help support the church. (Nevada Historical Society, wa00723.)

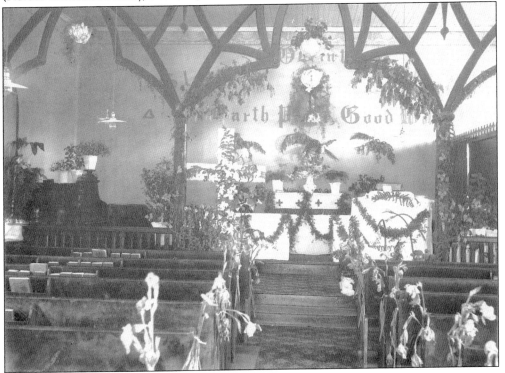

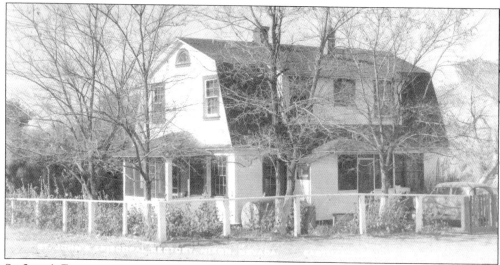

ST. JOHN'S EPISCOPAL RECTORY, NIXON. Joseph Hogben, a well-known "buckaroo" and saddlebag priest for the Protestant Episcopal parish, made his rounds to his church members at Pyramid Lake on horseback. The Wadsworth Protestant Episcopal Church was moved to Sparks in the 1920s. The St. Michael and All Angels chapel was built in its place as part of the Nixon parish. (Nevada Historical Society, wa09999.)

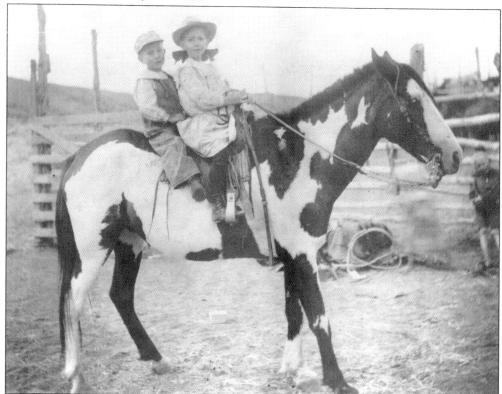

JEAN & FRED ESDEN. Children are out for a horseback ride on the Blundell Ranch in northern Washoe County in 1920. The Blundell ranch became the Monte Cristo Dude Ranch in the 1930s. (Nevada Historical Society, wa00739.)

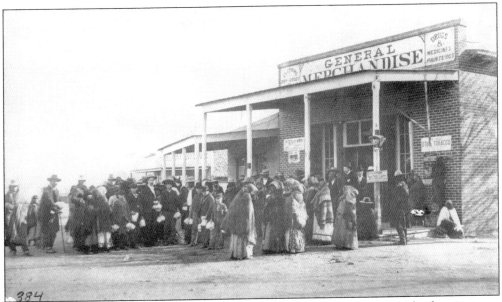

GRISWOLD'S STORE. Eugene Griswold's store in Wadsworth was a mercantile with advertisements stating that "E. Griswold makes a specialty of everything that is usually kept in a general merchandise store." Drugs, paints, oils, clothing, dry goods, tobacco, and liquor were sold. (Nevada Historical Society, eth00384.)

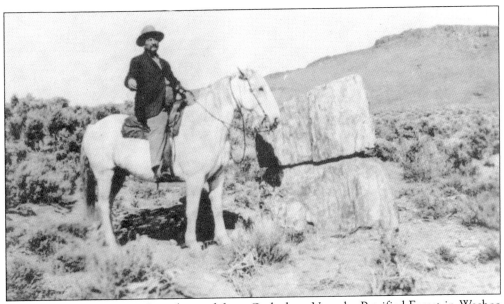

PETRIFIED FOREST. Located on the road from Gerlach to Vya, the Petrified Forest in Washoe County was described by an article in the *Nevada State Journal* in 1955 as "gigantic stumps of what was at one time an extensive grove if not actually a forest." This stump is six feet in diameter and eight feet tall. (Nevada Historical Society, wa06252.)

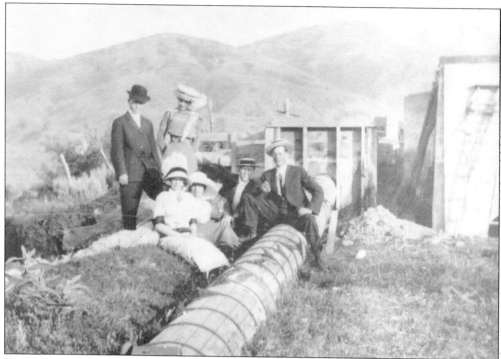

PICNIC ABOVE VERDI. The Lusty family is on an outing in the hills above the Truckee Meadows near Verdi in 1915. Peavine Mountain is in the background. The women, wearing lovely hats, are dressed in their Sunday best. Grace Lusty is in front and Edward Lusty, a pharmacist in Reno and in Truckee, California, took the photograph. (Nevada Historical Society, wa04984.)

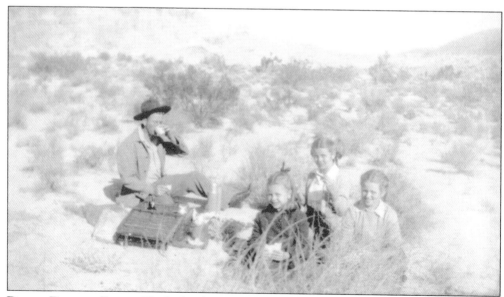

DOUBLE DIAMOND PICNIC. The Richardson family was having a picnic south of Reno in a sagebrush field at the Double Diamond Ranch in the 1940s. (Nevada Historical Society, wa04371.)

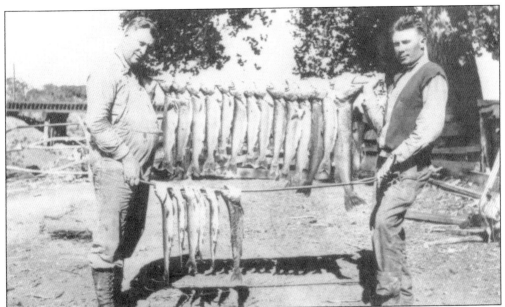

FISHING AT PYRAMID LAKE. Pyramid Lake cutthroat trout, a subspecies of the Lahontan cutthroat trout, could grow up to four feet in length. Beginning in 1869, these fish were shipped from Wadsworth to San Francisco markets. Fremont described the fish in his journal of 1844 as "flavor was excellent—superior, in fact, to any fish I have ever known." The largest fish caught in Pyramid Lake was a 41.5-pound cutthroat trout caught by Johnny Skimmerhorn in 1925. (Nevada Historical Society, wa04599.)

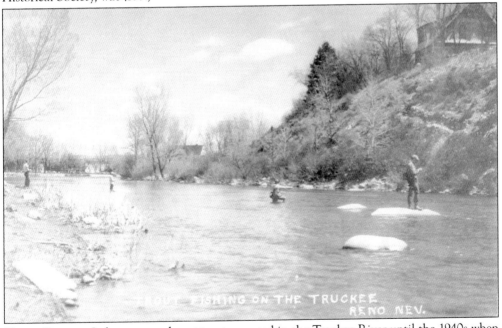

TROUT FISHING. Lahontan cutthroat trout spawned in the Truckee River until the 1940s when overfishing and dam construction caused a reduction of their numbers. An article in the *Territorial Enterprise* on March 20, 1869, said, "White men and Indians with hook and line, spear and net are busy catching the speckled beauties, for fun and for profit." (Southerland Collection.)

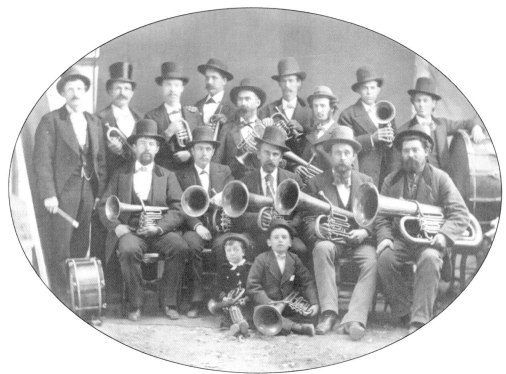

WADSWORTH BAND. Residents in Wadsworth celebrated their library, built in April 1884, with music by the Wadsworth Band. The library was described as a "fine collection of books and commodious building." The Wadsworth Band played for a surprise party for Mr. and Mrs. Patsy Gillispie with music described as "discoursed sweet music." (Nevada Historical Society, wa00742.)

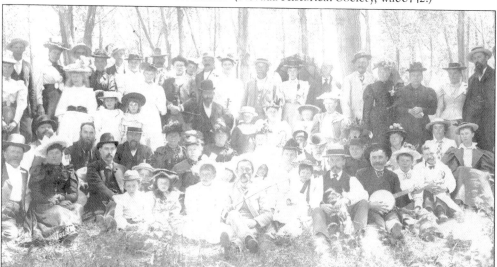

STEAMBOAT SPRINGS PICNIC. The hot springs at Steamboat Springs were developed as a health resort when James Cameroon opened a hotel in 1860. An article in the 1950 *Nevada State Journal* reported, "During the gaudy and fabulous days of the Comstock it was one of the favorite play spots for the big operators and its walls rang with their whoops and carousals." (Nevada Historical Society, wa05348.)

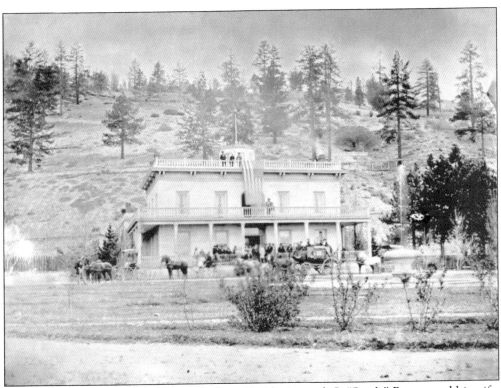

BOWERS MANSION. Bowers Mansion, built in 1864 by Lemuel. S. "Sandy" Bowers and his wife, Allison "Eilley" Orrum, was on 54 acres of land in Franktown. The property included a carriage house, dove house, greenhouse, and large dancing hall. The mansion was reported to cost from $200,000 to $400,000. It was made of cut stone and was supposed to have gold doorknobs and hinges. Mirrors that cost $3,000 and lace curtains that cost $1,200 were in each room. (Nevada Historical Society, wa00042.)

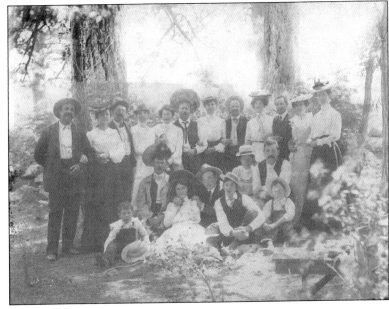

PICNIC AT BOWERS MANSION. This group was having a picnic at Bowers Mansion in the 1900s. Bowers Mansion became the gathering place for picnics and celebrations after it was bought and renovated in 1903 by Henry Riter, a Reno saloonkeeper and brewer. (Nevada Historical Society, wa00080.)

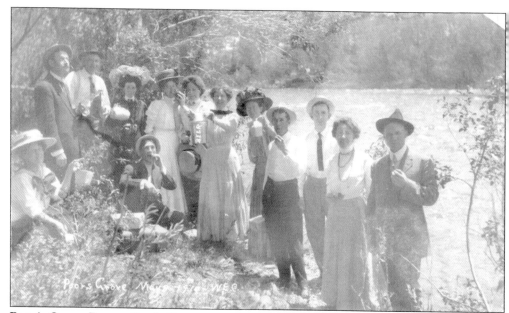

POOR'S GROVE PICNIC. Poor's Grove was renamed the Riverside Pleasure Park in 1905. Sunday afternoon concerts were planned with a new dancing pavilion and grandstand. A 10¢ bus fare brought people from Reno to the park each half hour. Poor's Grove became Idlewild Park. (Nevada Historical Society, wa03456.)

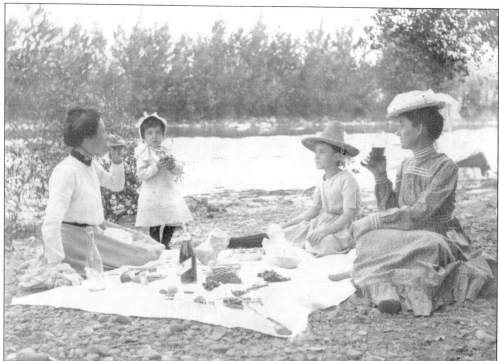

PICNIC BY RIVER. This group is having a picnic beside the Truckee River near Pyramid Lake in 1898. A blanket is spread on the riverbank and the family is eating grapes and pretzels. (Nevada Historical Society, wa00420.)

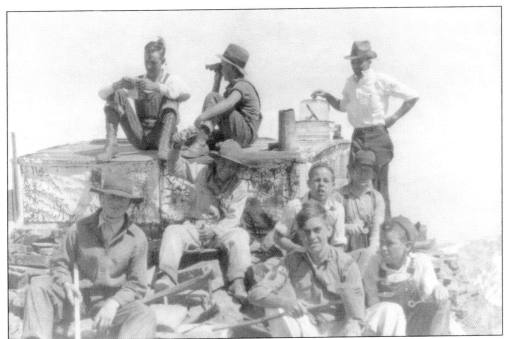

WEATHER HUT. A group is picnicking at the Mount Rose Weather Observatory on the summit of Mount Rose in 1932. Some of those in the photograph are Dellus Richins, Hugh Widamen, Tom O'Sullivan, Hardyn Vidovich, Roy Porter, Newell F. Wasdin, and Olivis F. Hansen. (Nevada Historical Society, wa05311.)

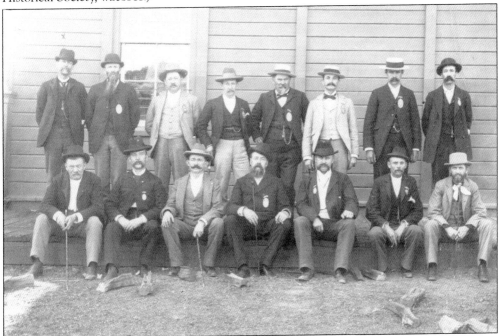

KNIGHTS OF PYTHIAS. The Wadsworth Knights of Pythias organization is shown in 1905. Established in 1864 in Washington, DC, the Knights of Pythias are a fraternal organization known for their "friendship, charity, and benevolence." (Nevada Historical Society, wa01087.)

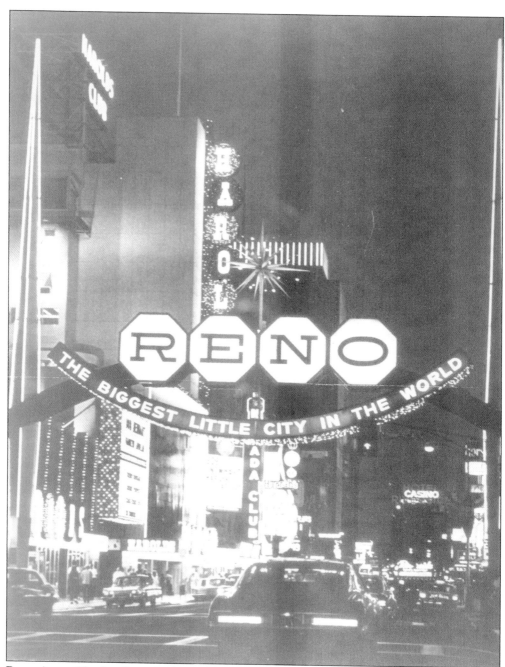

Reno Arch. The first Reno Arch was built to celebrate the completion of the Victory Highway (US 40) and Lincoln Highway (US 50) in 1927. The winning slogan, "The Biggest Little City in the World," placed on the arch was submitted by G.A. Burns, a resident of Sacramento, in a contest in 1929. The dedication of this 1963 arch was made at 10:00 pm on New Year's Eve. Mayor Hugh Quilici of Reno pulled the handle of a slot machine that was designed to flip the switch to light the arch. The arch was financed by casino owners on Virginia Street. The dedication of this arch was held in conjunction with the Nevada Centennial Commission. (Nevada State Library and Archives, PLA-0188.)

Six

WATER AND POWER

Water, needed for the livelihood of early Washoe County residents, was hard to come by. Washoe County receives about seven inches of rain per year with a high, dry desert climate with temperatures in the upper 80s and 90s during the summer and below freezing during the winter.

The old saying, "Whiskey is for drinking, water is for fighting over" describes Washoe County's water situation. Sawmills and quartz mills used water for power generation and to flume timber from the mountains. According to *Water in Nevada*, published by the Nevada Division of Water Resources, agricultural production was dependent on proximity to the mining camps. From 1849 to 1860, if the mining camp needed agricultural products, irrigation water was made available to ranches and farms.

Lake Tahoe, the largest body of water in the county, feeds into the Truckee River, bringing water to Washoe County. The Truckee River flows 105 miles from Lake Tahoe, entering Washoe County near Verdi, then ending at Pyramid Lake 40 miles northeast of Reno. When the first settlers needed water, they would just dig a ditch connecting their property to the Truckee River. Later, ditch users formed companies to administer their ditch agreements. The Pioneer Ditch near the current Greg Street Bridge and the Cochrene (Cochran) Ditch near Wingfield Park were the first ditches to be built in the 1860s, followed by the Longley, English Mill, Sessions, North Truckee, and Lake Ditches. A law in effect in 1866 required anyone constructing a ditch or flume to file a certificate with the county recorder giving the area served by the ditch and the name of the ditch.

The first electricity to come to Washoe County and to Nevada was by way of the Reno Electric Light and Power Company in 1882. Power for the steam plant was generated by wood and coal.

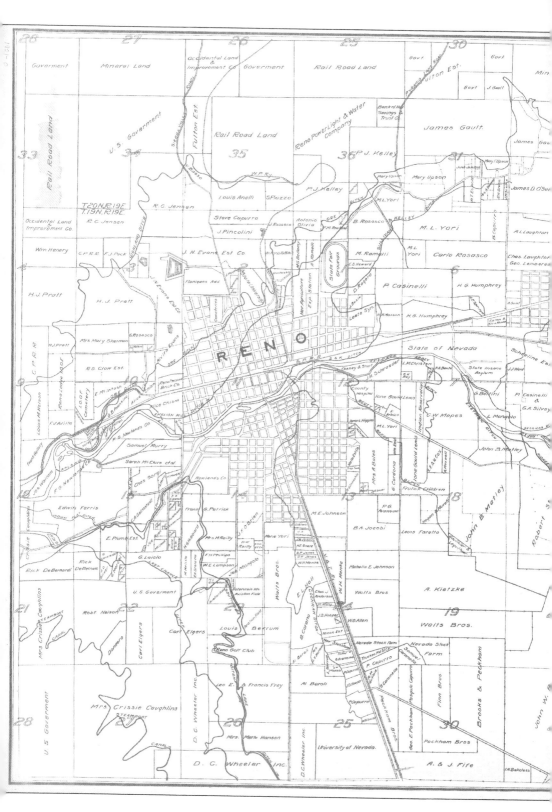

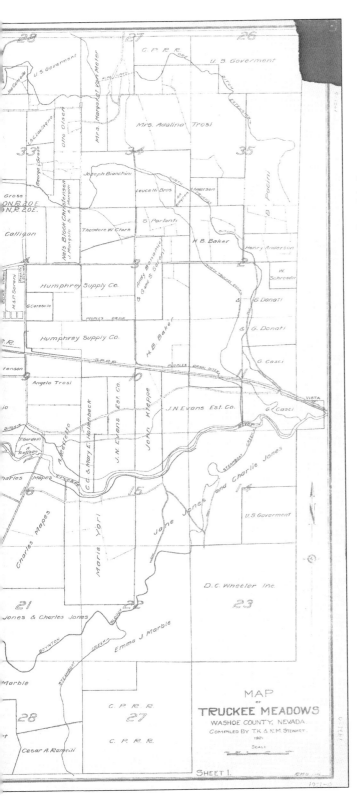

TRUCKEE MEADOWS WATER MAP. A map drawn in 1921 shows the location of some of the ranches in the Truckee Meadows with the irrigation ditches and streams that were used by each ranch. The Pioneer Ditch, the first ditch in the Truckee Meadows, brought water to the farms near Steamboat Creek in the mid-1860s. The Truckee Ditch was 17 miles long, stretching from the Mayberry Bridge to Brown's Station. Other major ditches were the Sullivan Ditch, North Truckee Ditch, Sessions Ditch, Glendale Ditch, Highland Ditch (1875), English Mill Ditch (1865), Indian FlatDitch, Cochrene (Cochran) Ditch (1860s), Mayberry Ditch, Abbey Ditch, Hunter Creek (1863), and Steamboat Ditch. The Orr Ditch, more than 20 miles long, brought water to the Spanish Springs Valley. The Steamboat Ditch, completed in 1880, was 23 miles long, providing water to Steamboat and Pleasant Valley. The Highland Ditch, a 14-mile ditch from Peavine Creek to High Reservoir, was built in 1888. It became the primary source of water for the city of Reno. (Nevada Historical Society.)

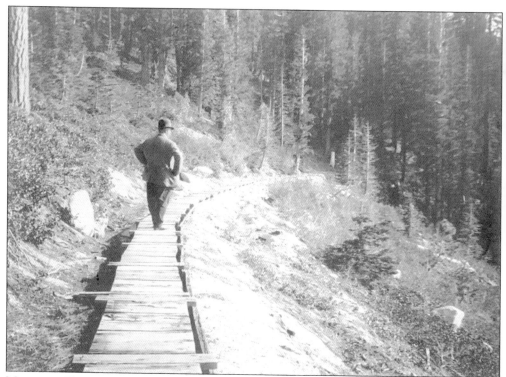

MARLETTE FLUME. Completed in 1875 to bring water from Lake Tahoe to Virginia City, the Marlette Lake Flume by 1887 was a series of box flumes that were more than 46 miles in length. Water came from Marlette Lake, Hobart Creek Reservoir, and Five-Mile Reservoir to pressure pipes in Washoe Valley to Virginia City and Gold Hill. A state inspector is examining the flume in 1913. (Nevada State Library and Archives, H20-0024.)

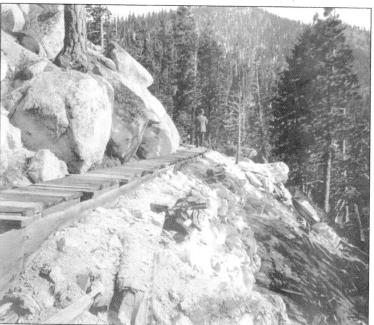

NORTH FLUME NEAR MARLETTE LAKE. This is a photograph of a treacherous section of the north flume near Marlette Lake in 1913. The *Reno Evening Gazette* reported in 1913 that the "flume dives into tunnel through the mountains which carries the water through to the easterly slope." (Nevada State Library and Archives, H20-0027.)

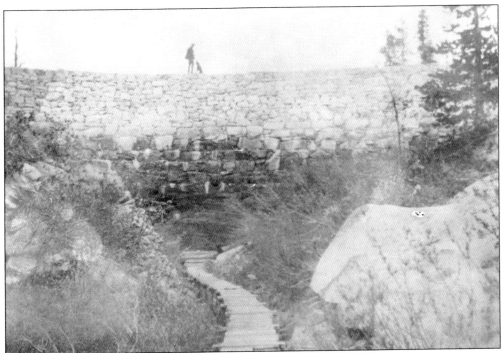

MARLETTE DAM. A dam was placed on Marlette Creek east of Lake Tahoe to provide water to flume logs to Washoe Valley sawmills in 1873. Marlette Dam provided water for mining camps in Virginia City in 1876 and later to state buildings in Carson City. This photograph was taken in the 1920s. (Nevada Historical Society, wa01134.)

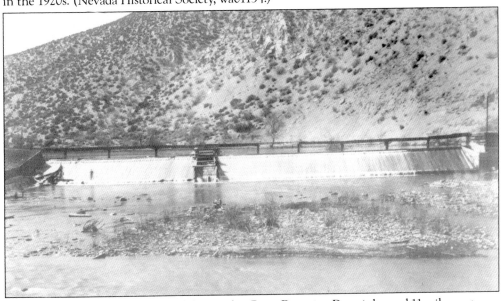

DERBY DAM. Derby Dam, first called the Truckee River Diversion Dam, is located 11 miles upstream from Wadsworth and was completed in June 1905 as part of the Newlands Project. Water from Derby Dam was diverted to a canal that went to the Carson River and, by 1915, to the Lahontan Reservoir. The dam reduced the water flowing into Pyramid Lake, and by 1969 the water level in Pyramid Lake had dropped 89 feet. (Nevada Historical Society, wa09550.)

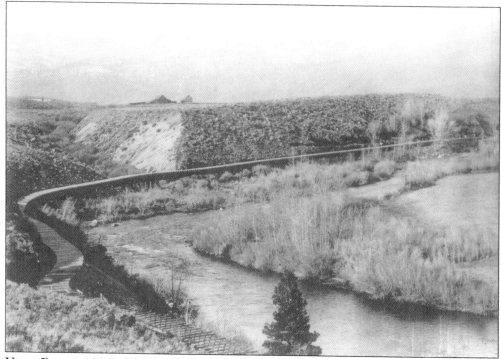

VERDI FLUME, 1900s. This box flume, built from two-inch-thick pine, was in Verdi in 1909. Water from the Truckee River came to Reno in this flume. The water in the flume was later used by the Truckee River General Electric Company to generate electricity. An article in the *Reno Evening Gazette* in 1911 reported that the power from the dam, flume, power plant, and canal was "capable of furnishing all the electricity needed in Western Nevada." (Nevada Historical Society, wa06976.)

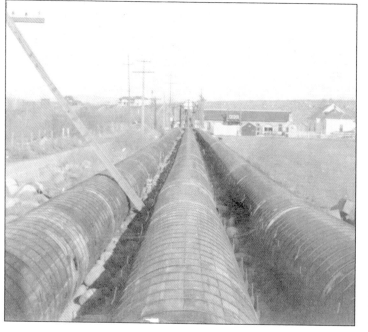

FLUMES AND POWER HOUSE. The Reno Water Land and Light Company built a hydropower plant in 1899. A Truckee River Power Company advertisement in a November 1923 *Nevada State Journal* said that the company had five "modern fully equipped hydro-electric plants on the Truckee." Water and gas service were provided to Reno and Sparks and, through a subsidiary of the company, to Carson City. (Nevada Historical Society, wa04001.)

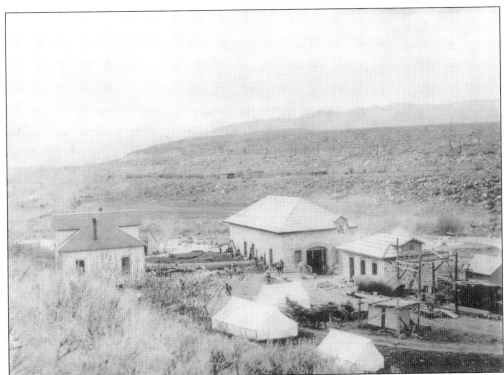

MOGUL POWER PLANT. This hydroelectric power plant was built in Mogul in 1905 by the Washoe Power Development Company. The Mogul Plant used 245,000 acre feet of water in 1969. The Verdi Plant, located near the Fleish Plant, was built in 1912 and used 225,000 acre feet of water in 1969. (Nevada Historical Society, wa06358.)

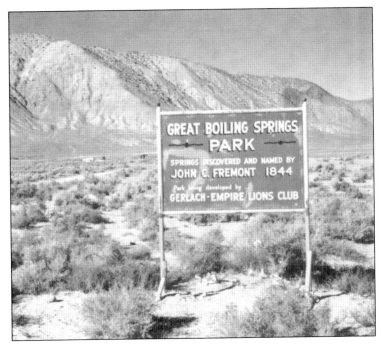

GREAT BOILING SPRINGS. John C. Fremont was thought to be the first white man to see the hot springs near Gerlach in January 1844. Washoe County voters passed a bond issue in 1962 for hiking trails and recreational facilities at Great Boiling Springs. In 1964, the springs were not considered a high priority for the county. (Nevada Historical Society, wa00915.)

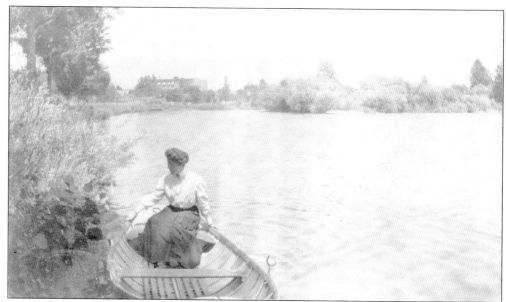

BOATING ON THE TRUCKEE. Fishing, kayaking, swimming, and rafting are some of the recreational activities now on the Truckee River. Here D. Maude is shown in a boat on the Truckee River in 1910. According to *Water in Nevada* in 1971, the Truckee River irrigated 18,000 acres in the Truckee Meadows and 1,700 acres in the Spanish Springs Valley. (Nevada Historical Society, wa03851.)

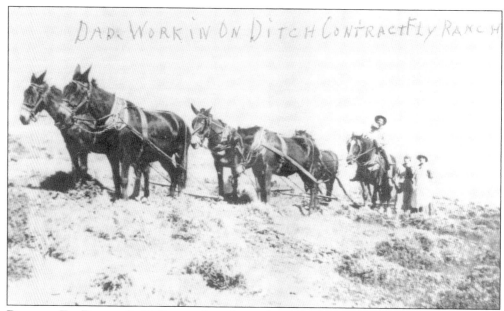

DITCH AT FLY RANCH. In 1910, a ranch worker is digging a ditch for the Fly Ranch in northern Washoe County, 20 miles from Gerlach. Fly Ranch is best known for a fountain or geyser that was caused by drilling a well. An article in the 1955 *Nevada State Journal* describes the fountain as "a shining, beautifully colored material kept bright by the water cascading down its sides, and from its peak a thin stream continually squirts upward into the air." (Nevada Historical Society, wa06601.)

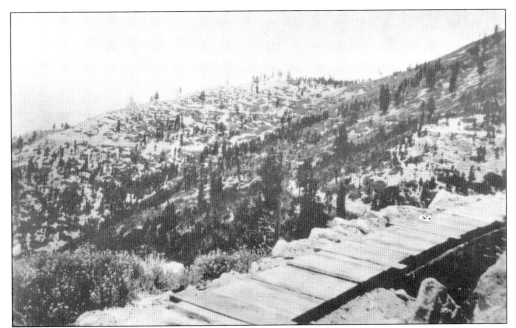

HOBART CREEK FLUME. There were four box flumes coming from Hobart Dam in 1873 to a pressure pipe system that was eight miles in length that brought water from Washoe Valley to Five Mile Reservoir in the Virginia Range. One of the flumes from the Hobart Dam was 18 inches deep, 20 inches wide, and 24,403 feet (or 4.62 miles) in length. This was the first water from the Truckee River Basin to Gold Hill and Virginia City. (Nevada Historical Society, wa1128.)

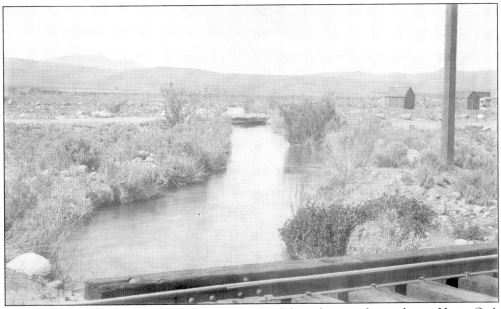

ORR DITCH. Built in 1863 by Henry Orr, the Orr Ditch brought water from a dam to Henry Orr's ranch, located two miles east of Mayberry Crossing, and later provided water for the growing city of Reno. By 1873, the ditch was extended to the ranches north and east of Reno in Spanish Springs Valley. The Orr Ditch Decree of 1944 adjudicated water rights from the Truckee River within Nevada. (Nevada Historical Society, wa01004.)

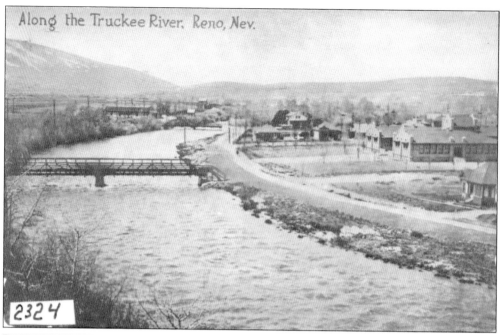

TRUCKEE RIVER, 1906. First named the Salmon Trout River by John C. Fremont in 1844, the river's name was changed to Truckee later that year in honor of an Indian guide for an emigrant party. The Truckee River was and is still the main source of water for irrigation for the ranches in Washoe County. (Nevada Historical Society, wa02324.)

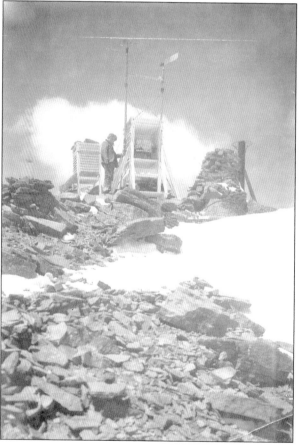

DR. CHURCH'S WEATHER OBSERVATORY. The Weather Observatory built on the Mount Rose Summit in 1905 by Dr. James Edward Church was a high mountain weather station to study climate and snow levels in the Sierra Nevada. Dr. Church constructed a snow sampler that accurately measured the amount of snow and its water content. (Nevada Historical Society, wa00954.)

BIBLIOGRAPHY

Carlson, Helen S. *Nevada Place Names*. Reno, NV: University of Nevada Press, 1974.

Handbook of Northern American Indians, vol. 11. Washington, DC: Smithsonian Institution, 1978.

Hermann, Ruth. *Paiutes at Pyramid Lake: A Narrative Concerning A Western Nevada Indian Tribe*. San Jose, CA: Harlan-Young Press, 1972.

Horton, Gary A. *Truckee River Chronology: A Chronological History of Lake Tahoe and the Truckee River and Related Water Issues*. Carson City, NV: Nevada Division of Water Planning, 1997.

Hummel, N.A. *General History and Resources of Washoe County*. Reno, NV: Sagebrush Press, 1969.

McGee, William and Sandra. *The Divorce Seekers: A Photo Memoir of a Nevada Dude Wrangler*. St. Helena, CA: BMC Publications, 2004.

McDonald, Russell W. *History of Washoe County*. Reno, NV: Board of County Commissioners of Washoe County, 1982.

Ratay, Myra Sauer. *Pioneers of the Ponderosa: How Washoe Valley Rescued the Comstock*. Sparks, NV: Western Print & Publishing Co., 1973.

Townley, John M. *Alfalfa County: Nevada Land, Water & Politics in the 19th Century*. Reno, NV: Agricultural Experiment Station, Max C. Fleischmann College of Agriculture, University of Nevada, Reno, [nd].

Townley, John M. *Tough Little Town on the Truckee*. Reno, NV: Great Basin Studies Center, 1983.

Woon, Basil. *None of the Comforts of Home – But Oh, Those Cowboys!: the Saga of Nevada Dude Ranches*. Reno, NV: Federated Features, 1967.

Discover Thousands of Local History Books
Featuring Millions of Vintage Images

Arcadia Publishing, the leading local history publisher in the United States, is committed to making history accessible and meaningful through publishing books that celebrate and preserve the heritage of America's people and places.

Find more books like this at
www.arcadiapublishing.com

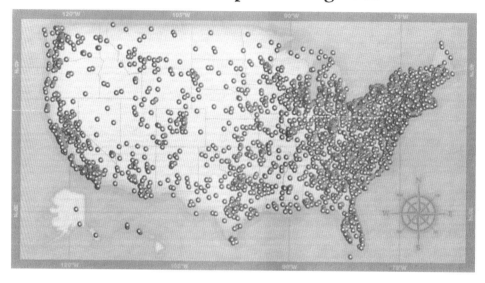

Search for your hometown history, your old stomping grounds, and even your favorite sports team.

Consistent with our mission to preserve history on a local level, this book was printed in South Carolina on American-made paper and manufactured entirely in the United States. Products carrying the accredited Forest Stewardship Council (FSC) label are printed on 100 percent FSC-certified paper.

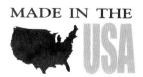